The Kind of Laws the Unions Ought to Want

Other Books by the Authors

Power at the Top: the Labour Party
   and its Public Corporations   CLIVE JENKINS

Power Behind the Screen: an Analysis
   of Commercial Television   CLIVE JENKINS

A History of the Association of Engineering and Shipbuilding Draughts-
   men   J. E. MORTIMER

Industrial Relations   J. E. MORTIMER

British Trade Unions Today   CLIVE JENKINS AND
                                        J. E. MORTIMER

The Kind of Laws the Unions Ought to Want

by
CLIVE JENKINS
and
J. E. MORTIMER

1966
THE QUEEN'S AWARD
TO INDUSTRY 1966

PERGAMON PRESS

OXFORD · LONDON · EDINBURGH · NEW YORK
TORONTO · SYDNEY · PARIS · BRAUNSCHWEIG

PERGAMON PRESS LTD.,
Headington Hill Hall, Oxford
4 & 5 Fitzroy Square, London W.1
PERGAMON PRESS (SCOTLAND) LTD.,
2 & 3 Teviot Place, Edinburgh 1
PERGAMON PRESS INC.
44–01 21st Street, Long Island City, New York 11101
PERGAMON OF CANADA LTD.,
6 Adelaide Street East, Toronto, Ontario
PERGAMON PRESS (AUST.) PTY. LTD.,
Rushcutters Bay, Sydney, New South Wales
PERGAMON PRESS S.A.R.L.,
24 rue des Écoles, Paris 5e
VIEWEG & SOHN GMBH,
Burgplatz 1, Braunschweig

Copyright © 1968 Pergamon Press Ltd.
First Edition 1968
Library of Congress Catalog Card No. 67–31504

Printed in Great Britain by A. Wheaton & Co., Ltd, Exeter

08 103691 4 (flexicover)
08 203691 8 (hardcover)

Contents

v

Introduction

THE purpose of this book is to argue the case for more legislation
to protect trade union rights and to establish or bring about
certain improvements in minimum labour standards. The authors
do not share the view, which is so frequently expressed in Britain,
that voluntary action provides the answer to almost all problems
in industrial relations. They believe that this view, when carried
to an extremity, is harmful to workers' interests. It has resulted
in serious defects in British law in relation to trade union rights
and it has contributed to the slow progress made in Britain—in
comparison with many other countries—in securing improvements in workers' conditions of employment.

It is not part of the authors' case to belittle the importance of
voluntary action. They are very much aware that the strength of
trade unionism depends in large measure upon the voluntary support given to it by working people. They also believe
strongly in the effectiveness of collective bargaining, particularly
when trade union claims are pressed firmly and when, if necessary, vigorous leadership for supporting action is given to the
membership.

But voluntary action and collective bargaining, as important
as they are, are not sufficient. A legal framework of affirmative
trade union rights is desirable, together with laws which will
establish certain minimum standards for all workers. In other
words, all round trade union activity requires a combination of
voluntary and legislative action. The TUC over many years
have already done much in this direction. The authors urge that
even more is needed.

This book does not cover the whole field of possible legislative
action on trade union rights and workers' conditions. Only a

few examples have been selected to illustrate the point of view which the authors hold. Other chapters could have been added, including one, for example, on workplace safety organisation. The authors are reinforced in their view on the need for further legislation by the introduction in recent years of a number of Acts of Parliament affecting industrial relations. Almost despite itself Britain has found it necessary to supplement voluntary action in industrial relations by legislation on such matters as the terms and conditions of employment in firms which are not parties to voluntary agreements, contracts of employment, industrial training and redundancy payments. The trend is there for all to see.

The authors hope that their book may contribute constructively to the public discussion now taking place on industrial relations.

CHAPTER 1

The surprising absence of a strategy

BRITISH trade unions have been successfully defamed. When it became clear that their bargaining power was growing they were criticised throughout the mass media by commentators and policy makers.

The campaign is now more than a decade old. Notable in it have been those newspapers and journals so sensitively orientated to the needs of an inefficient British capitalism that they organise protective diversionary raids before the captains of industry realise they need them.

Their representatives have attacked the unions on both television channels and been joined by the Conservative lawyers' organisations. The language has been extravagant. Usually, the descriptions of unions have resembled the specialised literature of the inclusive tour operator and the estate agent's advertisement.

There have been three main allegations. Firstly, the unions are too strong, too dictatorial and too greedy. Secondly, that they are so organised as to cling to all the old, inefficient methods of doing things and so have become the prime obstacle to modernisation. Thirdly, that they drive easy, cosy bargains with fearfully compliant employers in such a way as to victimise the unorganised consumer, particularly those who have no way of increasing their incomes.

The decibel count of this campaign has been extraordinarily high. It has certainly penetrated every editorial suite. This, of course, required no expertise and minimal guile; for there seems a tacit understanding between at least two newspaper groups to

1

translate their domestic tussles with certain printing unions into a broad outflanking attack on union institutions in order to weaken their own adversaries within their own establishments.

However, their first objective of resolving their problems to their own liking on their home territory has met with uncertain success. And, with their failure there, so has the volume of their attack on the wider trade union movement been turned up.

As the Goldwater camp's influence reached its apogee in the capturing of the Republican Party's Presidential nomination so did the newspapers' anti-union campaign reach its peak with the publication of the Conservative Party manifesto and the campaign speeches of the Conservative leader in the 1966 General Election.

The question of so-called "union reform" proved not to be a decisive issue. This was in spite of manufactured-in-bulk accounts of alleged union malpractices centring around the emotively titled "workers' courts" incidents in the Oxford and Reading parliamentary constituencies (where, as the Conservative members were subsequently unseated, it, at least, seems not to have been of measurable electoral benefit).

At worst, for the Conservative Party, it was a disadvantageous ploy which cost them support while obviously not mobilising (or exciting) their solid strength.

There was a notable increase in the support given to Labour candidates by white-collar workers. Significantly these same groups of workers are joining specialised trade unions in increasing numbers.

But the steady reiteration of the allegations *has* won its successes. There are even Labour politicians who accept that the unions should be cross-examined and asked to explain why they seem to be loitering with intent.

Some of these are lawyers who share with their Conservative colleagues in the courts the simple desire to have all the delicate and complex issues in collective bargaining dealt with by the judges, and the childlike belief that this is possible.

The very creation of a Royal Commission on Trade Unions and Employers' Associations was a victory for the lobby that called for it. There might be a case for appraising the vertical Gothic splendours of some employers' federations. But where was the evidence which compelled a review—obviously on the basis that there was a case to answer—of *democratic* organisations as opposed to the war machines of the owners? A frenetic rich political lobby created the Commission—not a clearly observed necessity for it.

Other currents in the Labour Party, which have shown themselves susceptible to influence by the thesis that the world of the unions is a jungle, are affected by—and rationalise—the feelings of some trade union leaders. The reason that the badly briefed and hostile critics have not had their arguments brought into fine focus—and disposed of—is that there is a crisis of confidence among some union leaders. Most of the unions show very moderate growth rates while some are in visible and accelerating decline —and some leaders don't know what to do about it. A nominally powerful union faced with technological change or competition which results in stalemate or catastrophic decline in numbers while others are growing in influence has morale problems within its *élite*. This has resulted, in some cases, in abdication of decision-taking of any moment and the acceptance of political initiatives from governments in order to maintain a sense of movement and involvement.

All could have been different and, in our view, must be yet. British trade unions should have a strategy. There should be a set of demands applying to all unionists to form a programme to be pressed for on every occasion.

All current national union programmes are reactions to external pressures. Unions, taken as a whole, and not excepting the Trades Union Congress at the centre, have failed to demand or make gains except of a minor nature and on a short-time scale of anticipation. Important, and long overdue, across-the-board reforms, such as compensation for redundancy, have had to be thrust upon reluctant and conservative union leaders who later equate all movement around them with their own efforts. Truly, in the absence of demands they have become the recipients of pressures and straightforward abuse and substantial intimidation—at least at the national level of official leadership.

The active membership, not in a position to research and elaborate policy, makes its points at annual conferences (or more infrequent meetings) or in the short run decisively with their own employers.

The malaise of the British unions stems not from greed. It is a product of their passivity and lack of appetite. While the weaker unions of other industrially developed countries have been making social gains the fiction has flourished in the United Kingdom that our bargains are best. In many ways this is an emasculating myth. In the absence of a positive "workers' charter" taken up by unions here on a broad front, the silent unions have been labelled as bodies working in a negative fashion, glorying in inflation and inflicting severe punishment upon members who dare defy despotic bureaucracies.

We repeat, such a description seems grotesquely false to a union member. But this is not to say he or she is satisfied. We detect a growing sense of dissatisfaction with their share of the product—and their exclusion from the decision-taking apparatus of industry. We believe they deserve new rights and that they would support an energetic campaign to win them.

A Charter of Workers' Rights

In the following chapters we urge that a charter of workers' rights should be adopted. This would provide a strategy for trade union advance.

Our movement's debates are hurried, shallow, inward-focusing, self-deprecatory—and unnaturally worried. We ask for confidence —and more.

We require nothing less than a programme for social justice in which the unfettered unions play a principal role in a democratic, voluntary way. But we need a new, better legal framework; this is the time to have that discussion and here are some propositions which might serve as building blocks.

The need is great, for with the passing into law of the two Prices and Incomes Acts in 1966 and 1967 the union movement was dealt a blow usually reserved for democratic institutions after the return to power of fiercely right-wing authoritarians.

The bankruptcy of the union response was inevitable after its long failure to frame new and exciting goals.

This situation must be reversed. This book is written for our friends; for while enemies may insist upon being heard friends may only ask. We are asking.

CHAPTER 2

Under-privilege in industrial relations

THE right of workers to combine in a trade union and to bargain collectively with their employer is a fundamental social right. It is no less important than the right of citizens to vote for the government of their country. It ought therefore to be the duty of the State to uphold the right of organisation and collective bargaining against hostile acts designed to prevent these rights from being observed.

For our discussion of British conditions it is essential to go back to first principles and restate the basis for our argument. In an industrial society, a worker is at a disadvantage when bargaining with an employer about his wages and conditions of employment. The employer is much stronger than he is. For as long as the worker negotiates as an individual this disadvantage remains—whether he is seeking a job or already in one.

The worker's resources are slender (an average working class household's cash reserves are not much more than £50). So if he is seeking a job and negotiating with a prospective employer he is conscious that he must find employment as quickly as possible. If he remains unemployed for more than a short period he and his family will soon be borrowing or contemplating an application for national supplementary benefit (which often happens during strikes).

If, on the other hand, the individual worker is already in a job and he is negotiating with his existing employer he is often sharply conscious that he is in a much weaker bargaining position than his employer.

6

He almost always, even during periods of labour scarcity, needs his job more than the employer needs *him*. In many cases the worker is tied to a locality and will be aware that there are few local firms, or possibly only one firm, where workers with his particular skill or training are needed. Should he decide to move elsewhere for new work he will be faced with costs which he can barely afford.

The livelihood of the employer or his agents, in contrast, does not depend on the employment of a single worker. He can afford to haggle in a relaxed way about the wage he is prepared to pay. When he is bargaining with an individual worker already in his employment he can, as a last resort, advertise for a replacement. If he is bargaining with a new applicant for a job he can wait for the next applicant if the first is not prepared to accept the terms which are offered.

When faced with this inequality of economic strength, workers have historically redressed the balance to some extent by combining together in a trade union. They can then confront the employer with a strength which would never be theirs were they to remain as individual workers in competition with each other for pay and job security. By combining together in a union and by agreeing to stand by each other in the event of a dispute with their employer they ease the competitive friction between themselves which is partly the source of their weakness when they stand as individual, unorganised workers.

Through membership of a union, workers are able also to secure financial assistance if they reach the point of breakdown with their employers. A union can accumulate a reserve fund which can be used to sustain workers during a strike or lockout, even though as individuals they may have little or no money on which to fall back (even though the strike pay in some unions is much too low). Money can also be raised by a union from other workers who are not directly involved in the dispute: it can also be borrowed.

This is the basic case for trade unionism in a narrow economic sense. It provides strength to workers to enable them to negotiate more effectively with their employer about the terms and conditions of their employment. To put it another way; the contract between an employer and an individual worker is not in reality a contract between equals, even though it may be regarded as such in law. It is only when the deal is negotiated by the workers collectively that something nearer equality between employers and employed is achieved. Even then, the overall settlements of the last 50 years have failed to change the proportions of the divison of national income between those who work and those who do not.* Without unions the share going to the workers would have declined.

The Responsibility of the State

It should be the duty of the State at least to protect the right of workers to organise into trade unions. If workers are denied the right to organise either by the State or by the actions of individual companies they will remain at a serious economic disadvantage in their relations with employers. This will reflect itself quite rapidly in their conditions of life. The terms and conditions of employment will certainly be worse than they would have been if the workers had been organised into unions, and social conditions generally will not improve as quickly as they should because of the absence of any pressure from a strong trade union movement.

There are, therefore, arguments of community interest and well-being to be deployed in favour of virile unionism. But how can the right of workers to organise best be protected? Undoubtedly, a very necessary—even the prime—requirement is the determination of workers *themselves* to exercise their democratic right to organise. There are countless examples throughout the history of the industrial system in Britain of the readiness of individual workers and groups of workers to make considerable personal sacrifice and endure hardship rather than succumb to the pressure

* For a much fuller discussion of this question see *The Theory of Wages* by K. W. Rothschild.

of either the State or employers seeking to deny them the right to combine for trade union purposes. *To this day in Britain the right to organise rests almost entirely on the independent strength of the trade union movement.*

There are some who argue that nothing more than the strength of the trade union movement is needed. They are suspicious of the intervention of the law because they think that the majority of judges and lawyers are prejudiced against trade unionism. They would prefer to keep everything out of the reach of the law so that issues can then be settled by the exercise of trade union strength and not by the decisions of the courts. The various attempts of the judges to erect dykes against the unions and invent novel hazards underline the force of this argument.

This line of reasoning is also reinforced from another direction. The settlement of disputes between employers and employed cannot be likened to the enforcement of law. There is no statute or common law by which the division of the product of industry between capital and labour can be determined. Each side believes that what it is claiming is "just" and "reasonable" and sometimes even "patriotic". The settlement of such disputes demands not a court of law but negotiators who, though conscious of their own strength, are prepared ultimately to effect a compromise and to strike a bargain.

Mr. George Woodcock, the General Secretary of the TUC, illustrated in a vivid way the difference between the enforcement of law and the settlement of industrial disputes in a speech on legislation to protect trade union rights which he made at the 1964 Blackpool Congress. A judge, he said, can make a decision and then go home confident in the knowledge that his decision will be enforced by others, including, if necessary, the police. Those engaged in industrial relations, however, have to live with their decisions. They cannot depend on others to enforce them. They have, therefore, to negotiate, to compromise, to accommodate the wishes of others, and to reach decisions which will be accepted by those in whose name the decisions are made, even though they may have reservations in doing so.

These are powerful reasons for keeping industrial negotiations generally out of the courts.* It is not part of the purpose of this chapter to suggest otherwise. Nevertheless, industrial relations do not and cannot exist in a legal vacuum. Every industrial State has found it necessary to create a legislative framework, seen or unseen, within which employers and unions can go about their business. The real argument, therefore, is not whether there should be legislation on industrial relations but what kind of legislation it should be.

The Legal Framework†

In Britain a legal framework already exists. It is formed by a very loosely linked series of Acts passed in the 1870's, by the Conciliation Act, 1896, the Trade Disputes Act, 1906, the Trade Union Act, 1913, the Industrial Courts Act, 1919, the Emergency Powers Act, 1920, the Wages Councils Act, 1959, the Terms and Conditions of Employment Act, 1959, the Contracts of Employment Act, 1963, the Trade Disputes Act, 1965 and the Redundancy Payments Act 1965. (It is an odd feature of the Ministry of Labour's Official *Industrial Relations Handbook* that in its index of relevant Acts of Parliament it does *not* include the Emergency Powers Act, yet this Act enables the Government to take far-reaching measures against a strike in a vital industry.) The interpretation placed upon these Acts by the courts is also very important, especially as some judgments seem to have whittled away some of the rights of trade unionists which it was the intention of Parliament to protect. Very recently, for example, the House of Lords in the *Rookes* v. *Barnard* case interpreted the

* However, it is only fair to note that when employers broke contracts following the passing of the Prices and Incomes Act, 1966, there were one or two cases where county court judges were willing to uphold the right of workers to receive money due to them under collective agreements. The money would otherwise have been pocketed by the employers.

† This section excludes the passing and implementation of the Prices and Incomes Act, 1966, with its penalties for the pursuit of certain trade union objectives. It is discussed more fully in a later chapter.

1906 Trade Disputes Act in such a manner as to undermine the right to threaten strike action. New law was created by the judges, and Parliament had to pass the Trade Disputes Act, 1965, to restore, at least partially, the rights intended by Parliament in 1906.

In the earliest days of the industrial system in Britain trade unions were regarded as illegal conspiracies. At common law they were held to be in restraint of trade and this violated the accepted doctrine of *laissez faire* which asserted that the good of society is best promoted by the free play of the market, without any kind of intervention from the State or organised groups. At the very end of the eighteenth century the common law was reinforced by the Combination Acts which prohibited the formation of trade combinations in all industries. This use of economic ideology for preserving basic inequalities was potent.

A first major step towards legality was taken with the repeal of the Combination Acts in 1824. An Act passed in 1825 imposed some new restrictions on the unions but did not restore the repression of the Combination Acts. For almost another half century after the repeal of the Combination Acts the unions existed without real legal status. From time to time they were attacked by the courts and found it necessary to defend themselves.

Legislation in the 1870's

In 1867 a Royal Commission was appointed to inquire into trade union activities and the possible reform of the law. It issued a number of reports all favouring the granting of some form of legal status to unions. Eventually in 1871 Parliament passed the Trade Union Act, based mainly on the recommendations of the Minority Report of the Royal Commission on Trade Unions.

The Trade Union Act, 1871, said that a trade union was not unlawful *merely* because its purpose was in restraint of trade. It also excluded the courts from enforcing agreements on trade matters, subscriptions, penalties or benefits, or agreements between one union and another. The Act also provided for the voluntary registration of unions with the Registrar of Friendly Societies. Unions which chose to register under the terms of this Act gained certain advantages relating, for example, to the holding of property.

But although the 1871 Act is sometimes described as a basic "charter of legal existence" for the unions, it does *not* say that workers shall have *the right* to organise and to bargain collectively.

In effect it goes little further than saying, first, that the unions are *not* unlawful bodies and, second, that the courts cannot enforce agreements relating to certain domestic arrangements of the unions or union rules or decisions for the maintenance of minimum wages and conditions. While the 1871 Act was a great advance it nevertheless had within it the defects which have become more apparent with the passage of time. It gave few positive rights to the unions and left them exposed to judge-made liabilities.

The 1871 Act was accompanied by another measure, the Criminal Law Amendment Act, 1871, which imposed severe penalties against persons who used violence, threats, intimidation, molestation or obstruction in order to coerce someone else for trade purposes. In a society less urbane than our own this was important. This Act seriously limited the right of workers to strike and to picket because it could be argued that even when they acted peacefully in pursuit of a trade dispute they were guilty of "molestation, intimidation or coercion"—and there were enough class conscious magistrates anxious to place the worst interpretation on the actions of trade unionists.

This Act aroused strong opposition among trade unionists and, following the report of a further Royal Commission appointed in 1874, was finally repealed. It was replaced by the Conspiracy and Protection of Property Act, 1875. The effect of this Act was to permit peaceful picketing in a trade dispute. It declared that an act done in combination in furtherance of a trade dispute was not criminal unless the act itself when done by one person would have been a crime. It was thus the intention of the Act to remove the doctrine of criminal conspiracy from application to trade disputes. This was a welcome reform.

The Conspiracy and Protection of Property Act, 1875, also made it a criminal offence for a worker employed in the supply of gas or water wilfully to break his contract of service knowing, or having reasonable cause to believe, that his action would deprive other citizens of their supply of gas or water. This restriction was subsequently extended to apply to workers in electricity supply.

The Conspiracy and Protection of Property Act, 1875, does not, it should be noted, make strikes *illegal* in gas, water or electricity supply. If proper notice is given the strike is legal. What it does do, however, is to make a breach of an employment contract in these industries a criminal offence and not merely grounds for civil action.

The 1875 Act also makes it a criminal offence wilfully to break a contract of service knowing, or having reasonable cause to believe, that the consequence of such action would be to endanger life, cause serious bodily injury or expose valuable property to destruction or serious injury.

The 1875 Act still contained penalties for intimidation, the persistent following of other persons, the hiding of tools and the watching and besetting of the house or place of work of some other person. These provisions are capable of being interpreted—and have been so interpreted—in a manner which has made difficulties for trade unionists engaged in peaceful picketing in trade disputes. The non-unionist and the strike-breaker have too frequently been treated with tender concern.

A further Act was passed in 1876, the Trade Union Act Amendment Act, 1876, but it did not add significantly to the state of the law in relation to trade union rights. It made a number of minor alterations to the Trade Union Act, 1871. It amended the definition of a trade union to include unions which were not unlawful at common law.

Trade Disputes Act, 1906

The next major event in the evolution of the legal framework surrounding industrial relations was the *Taff Vale* case and the subsequent Trade Disputes Act, 1906. This, too, was concerned with the rights of workers and their unions in industrial disputes and with the liability of unions in legal action against their representatives. Again, it did not deal directly with the right of workers to organise and to bargain collectively. In the Taff Vale judgment —which arose from a railway dispute in Taff Vale, South Wales— the House of Lords held that a union under the Trade Union Act, 1871, was a legal entity and could be sued for damages in respect of actions committed by its representatives. The Taff Vale Railway Company succeeded in their claim against the Amalgamated Society of Railway Servants that injury had been caused to their business by the action of members of the union who had conspired to induce workers to break their contracts of service and to join the strike.

The effect of this judgment was to jeopardise the right to strike. Unions immediately became extremely reluctant to authorise a strike of their members and to undertake picketing if their funds were in danger from claims for damages by the employers. The hazards for active unions were greatly multiplied.

But, in the political situation of the time, the unions were not without influence. Following considerable trade union agitation and the appointment and report of a Royal Commission on trade disputes, the victorious Liberal Government of 1906 passed a new Trade Disputes Act. This Act had an important bearing on trade union rights. It established:

1. That acts done by agreement by two or more persons in pursuit of a trade dispute are not unlawful unless the act itself if done by one person is unlawful. The risks of civil conspiracy in a trade dispute were thus much reduced.
2. That peaceful picketing at or near where a person works or resides is lawful. By picketing is meant to attend merely for

the purpose of peacefully obtaining or communicating information or peacefully persuading any person to work or abstain from working.

3. That it is not unlawful, in pursuit of a trade dispute, for a person to induce someone else to break his contract of employment. A person is also protected against claims that, in pursuit of a trade dispute, he has interfered with the trade, business or employment of some other person, or with the right of some other person to dispose of his capital or his labour as he wishes.

4. That the courts shall not entertain actions against a trade union in respect of any civil wrong (tortious act) alleged to have been committed by or on behalf of the union. An exception is made in connection with civil wrongs connected with the use of union property. The union may then be sued through its trustees. Immunity exists, however, where the alleged civil wrong is committed in pursuit of a trade dispute.

Trade Union Act, 1913

The campaign conducted by the unions to obtain new legislation following the Taff Vale judgment brought them, as never before, into the field of political action. A number of unions contributed money to help candidates pledged to support new legislation for trade union rights. Twenty-nine Labour representatives were elected in the 1906 Parliament. Interestingly, all campaigns against unions seem to provoke a radical political reaction—in the end.

In 1909 a member of the Amalgamated Society of Railway Servants, W. V. Osborne, took legal action to restrain his union from spending money on political activities. He succeeded in his case. The House of Lords held that the objects of a trade union were limited to those set out in the Trade Union Acts and that these did not give unions power to collect and administer funds for political purposes.

This was a crippling blow at the unions which had become sensitive to the need for political solutions to some of their problems. The Osborne judgment was socially very unjust. To support campaigns and candidates favourable to new legislation for the protection of trade union rights was obviously a legitimate activity in pursuit of trade union objectives. To this day many private companies can and do make substantial financial donations to organisations campaigning for political objectives favourable to what the directors regard as the companies' interests—or even sometimes simply in accord with the directors' personal prejudices.

The trade unions campaigned against the Osborne decision. One effect of the judgment was to make the unions rely more and more on industrial action to press their grievances. It also compelled them to withdraw financial support from a number of Members of Parliament. One side effect of this was the introduction of salaries for MPs who had hitherto been unpaid. Without the payment of MPs, and with the Osborne judgment restricting the use of union funds, independent working-class representation in Parliament would have become extremely difficult indeed.

The argument raged on and eventually a new Trade Union Act was passed in 1913. This augmented trade union rights in two main ways. In the first place it gave the unions the power to include in their constitutions *any* lawful object, providing that the main purpose were those of a trade union. Unions were also authorised to spend money in support of the objects set out in their constitutions. An exception was, however, made with regard to "political objects". It was by this proviso that the Trade Union Act, 1913, had its second main effect on trade union rights. It stipulated that before a union can spend money on political objects prescribed in the Act it must first take a ballot of its members and secure a majority of those who vote to approve the furtherance of political objects as a purpose of the union. Secondly, any payments made by the union in furtherance of these political objects must be made from a separate contributory fund. Furthermore, any member who does not want to contribute to this separate fund has the right, after giving due notice, to be exempted from payment. But then he must not be placed, either directly or indirectly, under any disability or disadvantage—except in relation to the control or management of the political fund—*because* of his exemption to contribute to the political fund. A member who feels aggrieved by an alleged breach of rule relating to the political objects of a union has a right to complain to the Registrar of Friendly Societies. After a hearing the Registrar is empowered to give a ruling which is binding on the parties.

The unions were, and are, much, much worse off than limited liability companies when it comes to financing their political programmes. The new Companies Act, 1967, requires companies to disclose their contributions to political parties. It does not require them to conduct a ballot of shareholders to institute a political fund, nor to provide for "contracting-out". The political objects to which the Trade Union Act, 1913, applies are enumerated in the Act. Section 3 reads:

(3) The political objects to which this section applies are the expenditure of money—

(a) On the payment of any expenses incurred either directly or indirectly by a candidate or prospective candidate for election to Parliament or to any public office, before, during or after the election in connexion with his candidature or election; or

(b) On the holding of any meeting or the distribution of any literature or documents in support of any such candidate or prospective candidate; or

(c) On the maintenance of any person who is a member of Parliament or who holds a public office; or

(d) In connexion with the registration of electors or the selection of a candidate for Parliament or any public office; or

(e) On the holding of political meetings of any kind, or on the distribution of political literature of political documents of any kind, unless the main purpose of the meetings or of the distribution of the literature or documents is the furtherance of statutory objects within the meaning of this Act.

The expression "public office" in this section means the office of member of any county, county borough, district or parish council or board of guardians, or of any public body who have power to raise money, either directly or indirectly, by means of a rate.

The Trade Union Act, 1913, does not preclude trade unions from furthering political objects other than those set out above, providing they are in accordance with their rules. But, we repeat, there is nothing to stop any board of directors doing what it will without effective challenge. The unions operate in a goldfish bowl: the employers behind a two-way mirror.

The Trade Union Act, 1913, may be viewed from two angles. On the one hand, it provides a lawful method by which unions may pursue certain statutorily defined political objects and spend money contributed separately for this purpose. On the other hand, it circumscribes the rights of unions in relation to political activities. In effect it says that their normal machinery for taking policy decisions (e.g. an annual delegate conference) shall not have the power to decide in favour of political objects, but must be replaced for this purpose by a ballot of members. Further, it says, in effect, that a minority shall be able to contract-out of the obligation to support objects approved by a majority in the name of the whole union. This is less than democratic.

The trade union movement has generally accepted the arrangement of the Trade Union Act, 1913, probably because it has regarded the Act, and still regards it, as a settlement of a controversial issue which, if disturbed, might result in more disadvantages to the unions than advantages. When the Conservatives disturbed the settlement in 1927 in the Trade Disputes and Trade Unions Act their action was looked upon as a breach of an understanding. The unions protested strongly and worked for the repeal of the new Act. The 1927 Act, passed as an act of revenge following the General Strike of the preceding year, was a vehicle for the curbing of trade union rights, including the requirement that even after a ballot vote of the members of a union had approved political objects, those who wished to contribute to the political fund should each laboriously "contract-in" before contributions could be collected from them. The 1927 Act was repealed by the first majority Labour Government shortly after the end of the Second World War. This was a long overdue act of restitution.

Trade Disputes and Trade Unions Act (N. Ireland), 1927

An Act almost identical to the now repealed Trade Disputes and Trade Unions Act, 1927, is still in force in Northern Ireland. It restricts trade union rights in Northern Ireland in a number of ways:

(1) It declares illegal any strike that has any object other than or in addition to the furtherance of a trade dispute within the trade or industry in which the strikers are engaged. Thus sympathetic strikes can be declared illegal. It also declares illegal any strike designed or calculated to coerce the Government either directly or by inflicting hardship upon the community. This provision is so wide that many strikes could be declared illegal which in Britain, where there is no such statute, would be lawful.

(2) It severely limits the right to picket. Picketing which "intimidates" a person is made illegal. "Intimidation", however, is so defined that it can mean reasonable apprehension of business losses by an employer. Indeed, if this provision is rigorously applied the legal right to picket hardly exists at all.

(3) It prohibits established members of the Northern Ireland civil service from being members of unions catering for persons outside the service. Thus civil servants are permitted membership only of unions catering for the civil service. Moreover, under the Act such unions must not include political objects.

(4) It prohibits local or other public authorities from making trade union membership a condition of employment or from introducing a similar condition for employees engaged on public contracts.

(5) It requires contributors to the political funds of unions to "contract-in".

This Act reflects the continuing reactionary character of successive Ulster Unionist Governments.

Emergency Powers Act, 1920

A statute which, in special circumstances, can have an important bearing on trade union rights is the Emergency Powers Act, 1920. This was passed following a mining strike in 1920. It was strongly opposed by the trade union and Labour movement, though since that time the powers that it confers have been used in industrial disputes both by Conservative and Labour governments. The Emergency Powers Act empowers the Government to declare a "state of emergency" if it appears that "any action has been taken or is immediately threatened by any person or body of persons of such a nature and on so extensive a scale as to be calculated, by interfering with the supply and distribution of food, water, fuel or light, or with the means of locomotion, to deprive the community or any substantial portion of the community, of the essentials of life. . . ." When a "state of emergency" has been declared the Government may issue regulations "for securing the essentials of life to the community".

The Act provides, however, that no regulation shall make it an offence to take part in a strike or peacefully to persuade others to take part in a strike. The Emergency Powers Act also states that it shall not be construed to authorise the making of regulations empowering any form of compulsory military service or industrial conscription. Despite these safeguards the Emergency Powers Act gives the Government extremely wide powers, if and when it chooses to use them, to break a strike. On a number of occasions the Government of the day has used the powers given by the Act to introduce troops to carry out work normally performed by workers on strike.

The legal framework, on the facts above, seems frail although it has functioned; but issues that seemed settled within it have a capacity of being raised from morbidity by judges.

Rookes v. Barnard

The protection which the 1906 Trade Disputes Act gave to trade unionists was seriously damaged by the House of Lords' judgment in 1964 in the *Rookes* v. *Barnard* case. This case concerned draughtsmen employed at London Airport. Mr. Rookes was at one time an active member of the Association of Engineering and Shipbuilding Draughtsmen—later known as the Draughtsmen's and Allied Technicians' Association—and helped to establish 100 per cent membership for the Association in the design office of British Overseas Airways Corporation. Under an arrangement which exists in civil air transport the 100 per cent membership was "registered" with the management. In such cases it is the declared practice of the management not to introduce into the "registered" office or workshop anyone who is not prepared to join a trade union.

Following a difference of opinion about how an office grievance should be pursued Mr. Rookes left the AESD (later known as DATA). The union alleged that Mr. Rookes wanted some form of "direct action" to secure redress for an office grievance, whereas its local full-time official, supported by the majority of members, urged that a remedy should be sought through the normal negotiating machinery. Feelings rose in the office and eventually the members of DATA passed a resolution informing the management that unless Mr. Rookes was withdrawn from the office they would strike. BOAC then suspended Mr. Rookes and eventually dismissed him.

Mr. Rookes took legal action against three representatives of DATA: two of them were lay members employed at London Airport and the other was a full-time official. He claimed damages on the grounds that he had been dismissed from his job as a result of an unlawful threat, namely a threat to strike in breach of an agreement in civil air transport (to which DATA was a party) that there should be no strikes or lockouts. It was held that this agreement constituted part of the contract of employment of each DATA member employed by BOAC.

Mr. Rookes won his case in the High Court, lost the appeal in the Court of Appeal but won the further appeal in the House of Lords. The effect of this Lords' judgment was to endanger trade union rights which it hitherto had been assumed were protected under the Trade Disputes Act, 1906. Astonishingly, it re-introduced the civil wrong of "intimidation" into industrial relations. Moreover some of the judges in the *Rookes* v. *Barnard* case made it clear that in their view a threat to strike is normally not a threat to terminate a contract of service—which would be legal—but a threat to *break* the contract. Thus the Lords' judgment in *Rookes* v. *Barnard* does not necessarily rest on the "no strike" clause in the civil air transport agreement. A TUC pamphlet entitled *Rookes versus Barnard, Opinion of Leading Counsel,* put it this way:

> This means that irrespective of the terms of any agreement between a union and an employer or the incorporation of those terms in individual contracts of service the ordinary strike notice is a threat to commit a breach of contract and is therefore a threat to commit an illegal act which exposes its maker to the risks of an action for intimidation.

Such an alarming proposition called for prompt remedial legislation.

Trade Disputes Act, 1965

At the 1964 General Election the Labour Party promised that if they were elected to power they would introduce legislation to restore to trade unionists the protection which it was generally believed they possessed under the Trade Disputes Act, 1906, before the House of Lords' judgment in the *Rookes* v. *Barnard* case. In fulfilment of this pledge the Labour Government introduced a new Trade Disputes Bill in February 1965.

The new Bill stated that an act done in contemplation or furtherance of a trade dispute—within the meaning of the Trade Disputes Act, 1906—shall not be actionable as a civil wrong on the ground only that it consists of a threat:

(a) to break a contract of employment;
(b) to induce someone else to break a contract of employment.

The intention of the new Bill was thus to restore some of the protection removed by the House of Lords' judgment in the

Rookes v. *Barnard* case. In fact, it was not an adequately comprehensive Bill. Its drafters were told so at the time.

The Draughtsmen and Allied Technicians' Association and the Watermen, Lightermen, Tugmen and Bargemen's Union—who had been involved in a legal case centred on the London docks, *Stratford* v. *Lindley* (see later paragraphs)—submitted a joint memorandum to the TUC which made the following suggestions:

(1) That the tort of intimidation should be abolished altogether. The memorandum said:

> Lord Justice Pearson spoke of "this obscure, unfamiliar and peculiar cause of action". We are advised that for all practical purposes there has never been a tort of intimidation in the law of England. The existence of such a tort, now sanctioned by the House of Lords, has obvious dangers for the trade union movement. We have managed without it in the past and there is no reason why we should not manage without it in the future; no-one but Mr. Rookes has found it necessary to call this tort in aid in the past, no-one but the Rookeses and the Stratfords are likely to feel the need for it in the future. It seems to us, therefore, that there is no good reason why the Common Law mischief as well as the statutory mischief of *Rookes* v. *Barnard* should not be disposed of at this stage.

(2) That wider protection should be given to unions by extending the definition of a trade dispute contained in the Trade Disputes Act, 1906. The memorandum said:

> We wish to draw the attention of the General Council to the extent to which the position of a union and its officers may be endangered by a court ruling that a trade dispute does not exist. A court may refuse to recognise a trade dispute even when one is put before them. The protection of the 1906 Act is then withdrawn. It was conceded in *Rookes* v. *Barnard* that a trade dispute existed and that all acts of Mr. Barnard and his colleagues were in furtherance of the trade dispute. But what would have happened if this concession had not been made? We are advised, and this advice is confirmed by the impression of Mr. Doughty who was present in court at the trial, that if this concession had not been made the court would probably have held that not all the acts done by Mr. Barnard and his colleagues were done in furtherance of the trade dispute. In that event they would have been unable to rely upon the Trade Disputes Act.

(3) That protection should be given to unions against actions for conspiracy to commit breach of contract. The memorandum said:

The House of Lords decided in *Rookes* v. *Barnard* that a breach of contract is an unlawful act for the purpose of the tort of intimidation. They did not decide whether breach of contract constitutes unlawful means for the purpose of the tort (or indeed of the crime) of conspiracy. Lord Devlin said: "I have not been considering what amounts to unlawful means in the tort of conspiracy. I am not saying that a conspiracy to commit a breach of contract amounts to the tort of conspiracy; *that point remains to be decided*." It could be held that in practice many strikes involve a conspiracy to commit breach of contract, and it is most likely that such a conspiracy would now be held to be unlawful. An action for the tort of conspiracy might be barred by Section 1 of the Trade Disputes Act, but the words of that Section were plainly wide enough so as not to bar the successful action brought by Mr. Rookes, despite the decision of the Court of Appeal. Who can be sure now that there is anything left of Section 1 at all?

The General Council of the TUC also suggested an alternative to the Trade Disputes Bill, as it then was, when introduced by the Government. They suggested an amendment to section 3 of the 1906 Trade Disputes Act to ensure that an Act done in contemplation or furtherance of a trade dispute shall not be actionable on the ground only "that it constitutes or contributes to intimidation by a threat to commit, or to procure, a breach of any contract".

The General Council argued that the reference in their proposed amendment to "any contract", as distinct from the contract of employment, would cover the threat to procure the breach of a commercial contract in the context of a trade dispute. Furthermore, the General Council believed that by making a threat to break a contract no longer illegal the tort of conspiracy would no longer arise.

The views expressed in the joint memorandum of the Draughtsmen's Association and the Lightermen's Union and by the General Council of the TUC pointed to the limitations of the Trade Disputes Act, 1965.

The Trade Disputes Act, 1965, does not deal with trade disputes, which a court might hold not to be trade disputes within the meaning of the 1906 Trade Disputes Act. This is not merely a legal quibble. In the case of *Stratford* v. *Lindley* affecting lightermen in the London docks the House of Lords held that the union and its officials were not protected by the Trade Disputes Act, 1906, because there was no furtherance or contemplation of a trade dispute. In the *Modern Law Review*, March 1965, Professor K. W. Wedderburn said: "This astounding decision is, in a sense, the gravest aspect of the case, because so many liberties of industrial action depend still upon a reasonable interpretation of 'trade dispute'."

The facts in this case were that Mr. Lindley was, and still is, the General Secretary of the Lightermen's Union. This union, together with the Transport and General Workers' Union, had tried unsuccessfully on a number of occasions to obtain negotiating rights for its members employed by a barge operating firm, BK Limited, controlled by Stratford and Son Limited. The firm employed forty-eight men, of whom three were members of the Lightermen's Union. The others were members of the TGWU. The Lightermen's Union is, however, the predominant union amongst the barge operating employees in the London docks.

Eventually BK Limited concluded an agreement with the TGWU. The Lightermen's Union, in protest against the refusal of negotiating rights to themselves for their own members, then placed an embargo on the barges of Stratford Limited. It was this embargo which led to legal action.

It is true that the *Stratford* v. *Lindley* case was not a straightforward one concerning the recognition of one union by an employer. It involved the claims of two unions for recognition. If, however, one union objects to exclusive recognition for the other the dispute should still remain in the eyes of the law a "trade dispute". The rights and wrongs of the claims of the two unions ought to be settled by good trade union practice; but irrespective of whether a union is in the right or wrong according to good trade union practice it ought not to lose the protection of the Trade Disputes Act, 1906—and certainly not by eccentric judgments.

Early in 1966 another legal case confirmed the criticisms made only a few months earlier of the limitations of the Trade Disputes Act, 1965. The Emerald Construction Company (a small firm supplying "labour-only") secured an interim injunction against the

Amalgamated Union of Building Trade Workers. The union's officers had written to the main contractor on a site in these terms:

> It appears to us . . . quite clear . . . that your company intends to employ "labour-only" subcontractors without any regard as to whether brick-layers are available to meet the needs of your company by way of direct employment. . . . We feel that we have done as much as we can. Unless, therefore, the . . . sub-contractor is withdrawn by July 30, we shall have no other alternative than to withdraw the bricklayers already in your employ on the site . . . and reserve the right to take any further action necessary on any other sites.

This letter seemed reasonable against the background of a growing disquiet about "labour-only" contractors and "self-employed" workers (which is now being investigated by a Ministry of Labour committee of inquiry). However, it was not judged so and the building workers' union was restrained from achieving the objectives of union policy on the grounds that it was seeking to have a commercial contract, as distinct from a contract of employment, broken in its pursuit of these goals.

Trade Disputes and Contracts of Employment

The Trade Disputes Act, 1965, did not deal with the position of a worker who in pursuit of a trade dispute actually breaks his own contract of employment. It did not lay down whether such a worker is protected against action for breach of a contract of employment. More particularly it did not lay down whether the terms of a negotiating procedure agreement form part of the contract of employment of workers covered by it. If the terms of a procedure agreement form part of the contract of employment it could be held that a strike in breach of an agreement—for example a strike which takes place before the negotiating procedure is exhausted—is not only unconstitutional in the trade union sense, but it is also a civil wrong and can give rise to legal action.

If, on the other hand, a negotiating procedure agreement is held to be a voluntary arrangement for resolving problems between employers and union or unions it can be argued that a breach of the agreement does not constitute a breach of the individual worker's contract of employment. A breach of the agreement does not, therefore, on this interpretation provide grounds for legal action.

The second interpretation, namely that a negotiating procedure agreement is a voluntary arrangement not enforceable by law, is in accordance with the generally accepted practice for many years in British industrial relations and it is the preferable interpretation. When there are breaches of agreements the real task is to resolve the grievances and problems which have caused them; not to impose legal penalties on workers who have withdrawn their labour in pursuit of a trade dispute. The imposition of such penalties would solve nothing. It would only cause embitterment.

Those who urge that breaches of negotiating procedure agreements should be actionable at law usually overlook that many such agreements in British industry are one-sided. A TUC report in 1960 on disputes and workshop representation criticized many procedure agreements. It said: "If workers want a change to which managers object they must go without until the procedure is exhausted; but if managers want a change to which workers object the change stays while the procedure is being gone through." This is particularly infuriating if the issue is the dismissal of a union representative whose case is then seriously prejudiced by the delay.

It has sometimes been argued that the *Rookes* v. *Barnard* judgment derived from the peculiarity of the negotiating procedure agreement in civil air transport. The agreement, it is said, was understood by both unions and employers to form part of the contract of employment of each worker covered by it. Moreover, unlike most agreements, the civil air transport agreement contained an unconditional "no strike" clause. These points are valid, but no one can be certain that a court in the future will take the view that the negotiating procedure agreement in civil air transport was unique (or so peculiar) that the *Rookes* v. *Barnard* judgment has only very limited implications for other industries. Even agreements which do not contain an unconditional "no strike" clause usually have wording to the effect that there shall be no strike or lockout until the procedure is exhausted. A court may, therefore, hold that a strike in breach of procedure is a strike in breach of contract, even if proper notice of strike action has been given.

In the Second Reading debate on the Trade Disputes Bill, 1965, Mr. Gunter, the Minister of Labour, said:

> In the eyes of the law as it is today, as I understand it, a strike is a concerted withdrawal of labour in breach of contract.
>
> The only way to strike without breaking the contract of employment would be to terminate the contract first—that is, for those concerned to give notice and leave their jobs, which would break their continuity of service and might mean the loss of pension rights and other benefits.

This is an interesting interpretation of the law. If a breach of contract of employment is actionable, then by the Minister's statement many strikes could give grounds for litigation. Indeed, the only strikes which would be protected would be those in which the workers had first terminated their contracts—that is, to quote Mr. Gunter, "for those concerned to give notice and leave their jobs . . .".

Mr. Gunter's interpretation of what constitutes a strike was at variance with the original provisions of the Contracts of Employment Act, 1963. This Act distinguished between strikes which were and which were not in breach of a contract of employment. It certainly did not imply that the only way in which a strike could take place without it being in breach of contract was for the workers to give notice and leave their jobs.

Significantly, however, these original provisions were amended when the Redundancy Payments Act, 1965, was passed. Under both the Contracts of Employment Act and the Redundancy Payment Act no distinction is now made between strikes in breach of contract and strikes not in breach of contract. It appears that the Government's lawyers take the view that all strikes, except where notice to terminate employment has been given, are in breach of contract.

If all strikes are in breach of contract, except where notice to terminate employment has been given, so too are lockouts.* This, for example, was the view of the Draughtsmen's and Allied Technicians' Association when all its members in shipbuilding were locked out by their employers in March 1967. The Shipbuilding Employers' Federation gave notice to DATA that the employment of its members in federated yards would be suspended if the Association did not bring to an end an official strike of draughtsmen at Swan Hunter's yard on the Tyne. The employment of DATA members was not terminated, but only suspended. Some of them, for example those on monthly staff conditions, did not receive a month's notice of suspension. They received only a week's notice.

DATA did not offer a legal challenge to the Shipbuilding Employers' Federation. They took the view that to take such an issue to court might prove to be double-edged. If it were ruled to be unlawful to suspend a contract of employment during a lockout it might also be held to be unlawful to suspend a contract of employment during a strike. Clearly the present position of the law is unsatisfactory. It should be made to reflect the reality of industrial disputes. There should be no shadow of doubt about the legality of strikes and lockouts.

No Act of Parliament, of course, provides an absolute guarantee of trade union rights against the decisions of reactionary judges. This is not to suggest that all judges are social reactionaries; unfortunately too many are. It is worth remembering what Lord Justice Scrutton said in 1922:

> The habits you are trained in, the people with whom you mix, lead to your having a certain class of ideas of such a nature that when you have to deal with other ideas you do not give as sound and accurate judgments as you would wish. . . . It is very difficult sometimes to be sure that you have put yourself into a thoroughly impartial position between two disputants, one of your own class and one not of your class.

---

* Some lawyers might argue that it is doubtful whether a lockout imposed because of breaches of contract by workers was itself a breach of contract.

Employers' Views

Within the last few years employers' organisations have expressed themselves more sympathetically towards suggestions for
the legal enforcement of agreements, particularly agreements for
negotiating procedure. Perhaps the most clearly stated of these
proposals came from the Engineering Employers' Federation
in their evidence to the Royal Commission on Trade Unions
and Employers' Associations. Their propositions are worth
describing at some length.

The Engineering Employers' Federation stated that the collective agreements in the engineering industry covered a wide
range of terms and conditions and they did not wish to suggest
that it was necessary to contemplate that all these agreements
should be made enforceable at law. To introduce a system of
general legal enforcement in the civil courts would, they said,
involve making fundamental changes in the system of industrial
relations without any certainty that such changes would effectively deal with the problem of strikes in breach of agreements.

The Federation said that they did not consider it practicable or
desirable for employers to be put in the position of having to sue
their workpeople in the civil courts to secure the observance of an
agreement. Many employers, they pointed out, would be extremely
reluctant to take such action. Civil actions have their technicalities
and proof of damage may be complicated and difficult. But apart
from this there was the possible effect of such action on industrial
relations. Legal process was inclined to be slow in operation.

The Federation also pointed out that even in those cases where
penalties had been imposed by a court, for example, fines during
the war in connection with strikes in breach of the Conditions of
Employment and National Arbitration Order, it had been extremely difficult to enforce the penalty applied by the court. Obviously
the remedy of imprisonment for contempt of court for not paying
a fine was not practicable in relation to large numbers of men.

The Federation, nevertheless, asked the Commission to consider
whether certain more limited steps ought not to be taken to secure

that, when there were agreed procedures for the discussion of questions arising at works, strikes and other action to bring pressure on a company before these procedures had been fully used would be prohibited. Anyone taking part in such action would then render himself liable to penalty.

The Federation then went on to say:

> As already indicated, the Federation supports the proposals of the Confederation of British Industry relating to a registrar of trade unions with supervision over the rules of trade unions and particularly the suggestion that those rules might provide for certain penalties "in connection with unofficial strikes" [Para. (186(d)) of its evidence]. It believes, however, that this suggestion may not be sufficient and considers that it requires supplementing or replacing by a clear provision that workpeople who take strike or other action (e.g. go-slow tactics, bans on overtime and the extension of disputes by the "blacking" of work) to coerce their employer before the applicable procedural arrangements have been fully utilized and there has been no settlement of the issue raised, be made liable to the imposition by an independent tribunal of monetary penalties.
>
> The Federation suggests that there should be a tribunal to which, in the case of a strike in breach of agreement, complaint might be made against the unions concerned if they do not take all reasonable steps to prevent or stop such a strike.

The Federation said that it was of the utmost importance to emphasise the difference between unofficial strikes and strikes in breach of agreement. An unofficial strike, they pointed out, was one which took place in breach of union rules. Most unions, however, had power to declare any strike official, whether the agreed procedure for settling questions had been used or not. Accordingly, it was not suggested that penalties should be imposed in respect of unofficial strikes, since such penalties could be avoided by declaring strikes official. It was in respect of the strikes in breach of negotiating procedure agreements that penalties were suggested.

The Federation urged that it should be competent for a tribunal to impose a monetary penalty on a worker for every day on which he took part in a strike or other action in breach of agreement. They further suggested that such a tribunal should also have power to impose monetary penalties on unions if they did not take all reasonable steps to prevent or stop strikes in breach of agreement. The onus, the Federation said, should be on the union to prove that they had taken all reasonable steps. The Federation suggested that non-unionists who joined a strike of union members which they knew or ought to have known was in breach of agreement should be liable to similar penalties.

In establishments where there was no agreed procedure for dealing with questions arising (possibly because the company was non-federated or workers were non-unionists), the Federation suggested that it should be a requirement that before the workers concerned could be free to take strike action without penalty they must first seek the assistance of the local conciliation officer of the Ministry of Labour and that such intervention must have failed to produce a settlement.

The Federation said that employers should be required to publish in their establishments the details of the procedure agreements to which they subscribe. They also suggested a method for the taking of proceedings against workers.

> It is recognised that if an employer took proceedings, or the decision lay with him as to whether proceedings should be taken against his own employees, industrial relations in that firm might be seriously impaired. For this reason it is suggested that the decision to take proceedings, and the proceedings themselves before the tribunal, should be taken by the appropriate employers' federation to which the employer belongs and not by the employer himself. If the employer was not federated he might be empowered to take such proceedings himself.

The right to take proceedings would exist not only against unconstitutional strikes, but also against other "acts of indiscipline" when in breach of agreement. These "acts of indiscipline" were listed as "go-slows", bans on piecework, bans on overtime and the "blacking" of work.

Sympathetic strike action might also render workers liable to penalty, according to the suggestions of the Engineering Employers' Federation.

> It is suggested that sympathetic or supporting industrial action by workers outside the establishment where the strike or other action in breach of agreement is occurring, should also be subjected to similar penalties. Such industrial action consists, for example, of refusing to

handle goods or work on material from the establishment where the strike is occurring or of taking part in a sympathetic strike.

Finally, on the question of penalties the Federation had this to say:

> It is not envisaged that the amount of any penalty which can be inflicted should be automatic and predetermined. Justice would most probably be done if the tribunal had a discretion as to the amount of penalty inflicted.
>
> Any system of penalties which cannot, in practice, be easily enforced is of little value. It is accordingly suggested that any penalties should be deducted by his employer in instalments, as agreed or as decided by the tribunal, from the wages of the worker so penalised. If such worker changed his employer then a subsequent employer, on notice from the tribunal, should be bound to make the deduction from his wages.

The objective is clear. The engineering employers, unable to master the sophisticated and democratic arts of man management, want a State coercive power imported into the worker-employer relationship but without any stigma of blame attaching to a given plant management which can confidently call the Federation into play—rather like a common informer at work.

The Confederation of British Industries advanced views in its evidence which, if it were not for their essentially reactionary character, might seem remarkably innocent or naïve.

They, too, wanted to make collective agreements legally enforceable while, at the same time, not undermining "the principles of voluntary acceptance of responsibility". However, their document warned against "constant reference to the Courts or to labour tribunals" and ". . . the imposition of fines which might well not be paid." They added: "The Commission is invited to study further the possibility of combining such enforcement with other desirable features of the British voluntary system in a way which would substantially meet the difficulties listed above."

Essentially, the institutionalised employers called for repressive and intimidatory action against the unions, not because they think it possible to have such measures passed by a British Parliament in the late 1960's, but because they are pursuing the tactic of asking for more than they hope to attain in order to secure measures of *containment*.

A Political Intervention

They have been encouraged by the Conservative Party in this approach. The High Tory lawyers seem convinced that the courts *can* intervene in straightforward industrial disputes and settle them. In some ways the lawyer politicians are willing to go further than the embattled (and battle-scarred) industrialists.

The Minutes of a Conservative Party policy committee on this question leaked early in 1966.

Headed "SECRET" they ran, in part, as follows:

POLICY GROUP 20—TRADE UNION LAW AND PRACTICE

*Minutes of the 18th Meeting
held on Monday, 31st January, 1966, at 2.00 p.m.
in Interview Room J at the House of Commons*

Present: The Rt. Hon. Sir Keith Joseph, M.P. (*in the chair*)
Mr. N. J. Cooper
Mr. Aidan Crawley, M.P.
Mr. J. R. Edwards
The Rt. Hon. Joseph Godber, M.P.
Mr. Jack Hawkins
The Rt. Hon. Sir John Hobson, M.P.
Mr. Geoffrey Howe, M.P.
Mr. Ray Mawby, M.P.
Group/Captain P. G. Thomson
Mr. H. J. Williams
The Rt. Hon. Richard Wood, M.P.

In attendance:
Mr. Stephen Abbott

Apologies were received from:
Sir Max Bemrose
Mr. David Clarke
Mr. Frederick Garner
The Rt. Hon. Iain Macleod, M.P.
Mr. Dudley Smith, M.P.

1. *Penalties against Individual Strikers*
The meeting discussed the proposal by the Engineering Employers' Federation that fines imposed by the Courts against individuals might be deducted from wages.

The majority of members agreed that this was a practical means of enforcing Court awards against individuals and that the Group's Report should recommend that the proposal should be one for reference to the Royal Commission.

2. *Injunctions and Industrial Disputes*

Mr. Geoffrey Howe's Paper (PG/20/65/64) was considered. It was agreed that the use of injunctions might be effectively extended. The Group's Report should make reference to this as one valuable means of preventing unlawful acts—including breaches of legally enforceable collective agreements. It should, however, be made clear that this method should only be used in cases where it could be enforced in practice. It was unlikely, for example, to be effective in restraining thousands of individual strikers—acting without authority of their union.

3. The meeting then continued discussion of the Chairman's Paper (PG/ 20/65/60).

4. *Restrictive Labour Practices (Para. 7)*

The proposals contained in the Group's first Report were broadly accepted, and it was agreed that the following points should be stressed:

- (a) That after satisfying himself that a restrictive practice existed, the Commissioner should do everything possible to persuade the parties concerned to "desist"—before referring the case to the Industrial Court.
- (b) That, where this happened, the use of injunctions might well be the only effective means of enforceability.
- (c) That there would be clear limitations on the type of "practice" appropriate for reference to the Court. Some large-scale practices might not be suitable whereas others, of a less widespread nature, might be— especially if they were part and parcel of union Rules, working rules, or a written agreement between employers and trade unions.
- (d) That no strike called in protest against the abolition of a restrictive practice—in accordance with an order by the Industrial Court— should be protected under the Trade Union Acts.
- (e) It was for consideration whether the responsibilities of the proposed Commissioner could, as an alternative, be undertaken by the Prices and Incomes Board. . . .

5. *"Cooling-off" Period*

The meeting was generally in favour of legislation on American lines— where a strike could seriously harm the National interest. In such cases the Minister of Labour might be responsible for applying to the Industrial Court for an injunction to "cease and desist".

It was agreed that the Group's Report should recommend that this major departure from the U.K. system was something on which the advice of the Royal Commission should be obtained. The Party should not commit itself in advance.

6. *Collective Agreements*

After reviewing previous discussions on this subject it was agreed: (i) That legislation should provide that all procedural agreements, or clauses dealing with disputes procedure in comprehensive agreements are enforceable at law.

This Policy Group seems to have been drafting its own views for the Royal Commission and to have formulated a set of remarkably restrictive, interventionist and anti-democratic propositions.

Their extremism might well be their downfall: on the other hand, they provided the underpinning for the "union reform" declarations in the Conservative General Election Manifesto for 1966.

Statutory Wage Regulation and Trade Union Rights

The provisions for statutory wage regulation in Britain have a bearing on trade union rights. The principal Acts are the Wages Councils Act, 1959, the Agricultural Wages Act, 1948, and the Agricultural Wages (Scotland) Act, 1949. Statutory wage regulation has been applied to trades or industries where it has been held that voluntary machinery for wage-fixing does not exist or is inadequate and that in consequence "reasonable" wages will not be maintained. In plain terms, statutory wage regulation has existed to prevent the worst abuses of exploitation in "sweated" trades. In these trades there is often a large number of small competing employers, and the workers (many of whom often are women and youths) are usually badly organised in trade unions. Today about $3\frac{1}{2}$ million workers are covered by statutory wage machinery.

Under the Wages Councils Act the Minister is empowered to set up wages councils, after preliminary notice and inquiry, for trades and industries in which, having regard to existing wages, there appears to be no adequate machinery for their effective regulation. A wages council consists of members representing employers, members representing workers, and members who are "independent persons", all of whom are appointed by the Minister. It is the main job of a wages council to submit proposals to the Minister for minimum wages and for holidays and holiday pay. These are published and representations about them may be made to the Minister by workers or employers. The Minister, after considering any representations which he receives, may either make a wage regulation order to give the proposals legal effect, or he may refer the proposals back to the council for further consideration and possible amendment.

There are numbers of inspectors appointed by the Minister of Labour to enforce the legal requirements of the Wages Councils Act. An employer who is convicted of paying less than the statutory minimum wage can be ordered to pay the arrears for a period not exceeding 2 years. A worker may also take civil proceedings to recover arrears of wages if he has been paid less than the statutory minimum.

This activity is the ambulance work of an industrialised society. But the provisions for statutory wage regulation do not guarantee the right to organise to the workers covered by wages councils. The most that can be said is that their existence is likely to encourage organisation. In one sense, however, they do confer an indirect legal right to bargain collectively for workers who are in unions whose representatives sit on wages councils. But it is a limited and conditional right, one made in special circumstances and based on union weakness. There is no guarantee of the right to bargain collectively at workshop level where it *might* be real and *might* count.

Public Bodies and Trade Union Rights

In the nationalised industries a statutory obligation is placed upon the various public boards to establish machinery for the settlement of the terms and conditions of employment and, in some cases, to establish arrangements for joint consultation with employees on matters of mutual interest and on their health, welfare and safety. The wording of the relevant sections vary slightly from one nationalising statute to another, but the general principle is much the same. It is to the effect that each public board should establish negotiating and consultative machinery with appropriate organisations representing its employees.

The Acts do not specify what are the appropriate organisations. This is a matter for each public board to decide. This formula has meant, in practice, that the established trade unions have generally been able to gain recognition without difficulty, but a safeguard has been provided against the public boards having to concede claims for recognition from breakaway or non-bona-fide organisations which might have the effect of disrupting normal collective bargaining relationships.

Under the Education Act, 1944, and under the Fire Services Acts, provision is made for arrangements for determining the salaries of teachers and members of fire brigades. The provisions envisage that representatives of teachers and members of fire brigades shall participate in these arrangements.

Thus in the nationalised industries and certain public services there is what amounts to statutory recognition of the right of workers to bargain collectively through appropriate organisations. This means a virtual obligation on the employer to bargain in return—and in good faith.

The Fair Wages Resolution

The Fair Wages Resolution of the House of Commons also has a bearing on the right of workers to organise in trade unions. The first Fair Wages Resolution was adopted by the House of Commons in 1891, the second in 1909 and the current one in 1946. The Resolution is not an Act of Parliament and has, therefore, no statutory force. It is, nevertheless, a clear expression of the opinion of Parliament which successive governments have observed in their dealings with employers on government contracts.

The 1946 Resolution deals mainly with the requirement that contractors shall observe terms and conditions established by collective bargaining for their trade or industry; or, in the absence of such established standards, terms and conditions which are not less favourable than the general level of wages, hours and conditions observed by other employers whose general circumstances in the trade or industry in which the contractor is engaged are similar. The contractor is required to observe "fair" conditions as well as "fair" wages and to apply them to all workers in every workplace where the contract is being executed. He is also responsible for ensuring that the intention of the Resolution is observed by sub-contractors.

Section 4 of the Fair Wages Resolution of 1946, states: "The contractor shall recognise the freedom of his workpeople to be members of trade unions." If a complaint is received that a contractor is not observing the requirements of the Fair Wages Clause the Minister is required, if it is not otherwise disposed of, to refer it for decision to an independent tribunal—the Industrial Court.

The right of recognition is not accorded by the Resolution: a contractor on government work does not have to recognise a union clearly representative of his workforce—let alone bargain with their representatives. Sanctions seem only applicable if the contractor refuses to allow his workers to join or remain in a union.

In a case personally known to one of the authors of this book an incident of managerial persuasion of workers not to join a union was not given weight by the Industrial Court (because the company declared this was not its policy). Victimisation is also difficult to prove and overt acts are rarer than they were. The protection of the Resolution is limited.

The principle of the Resolution has also been embodied in a number of Acts of Parliament which provide some form of financial assistance to industry. Among such Acts, which contain a clause relating to the terms and conditions of employment of persons employed in the industry concerned, are the Road Traffic Act, 1930, the Road and Rail Traffic Act, 1933, the Road Haulage Wages Act, 1938, the Cinematograph Film Acts, the Civil Aviation Act, 1949, certain Housing Acts, the Television Act, 1954 and the Sugar Act, 1956.

Other Statutes and Trade Union Rights

The Conciliation Act, 1896, and the Industrial Courts Act, 1919, though an essential part of the legal framework for industrial relations in Britain, are not primarily concerned with trade union rights. They provide a means for conciliation, voluntary arbitration and inquiry into industrial disputes. These provisions are designed to encourage industry to settle its own problems, and to establish and to maintain joint machinery between employers and unions for the settlement of terms and conditions of employment. The services provided by the Minister help, on occasions, to obtain for workers the right to organise and to bargain collectively. It is not, however, within the power of the Ministry of Labour to compel an employer to recognise a union or to bargain with it. There are many big firms which actively discourage trade union organisation among their white collar staff.*

Under the Terms and Conditions of Employment Act, 1959, workers through their unions have a means of enforcing terms and conditions of employment established in any trade or industry between representative organisations of both sides. But this is a recourse of last resort.

If a union is of the view that a particular employer is not observing the terms or conditions of employment for the industry in which he is engaged it has the right to invoke, through the Minister of Labour, the adjudication of the Industrial Court. Unlike other disputes which are referred to the Industrial Court for arbitration, issues reported to the Minister of Labour under the Terms and Conditions of Employment Act can be referred to the Court *without* the consent of the employer. If the Court finds in favour of the claim the employer is required to observe the recognised terms and conditions of employment. An award of the Industrial Court becomes an implied term of the contract of employment of the workers covered by it and can, if necessary, be enforced by the workers in a normal court of law. This procedure cannot, however, be used to enforce trade union recognition.

* *Trade Union Growth and Recognition* by G. S. Bain, Research Paper No. 6, Royal Commission on Trade Unions and Employers' Associations (HMSO).

CHAPTER 3

Why not a legal right
to organise and bargain collectively ?

UNITED KINGDOM legislation on industrial relations, as has been demonstrated, does not present a coherent pattern. Laws have been passed from time to time to deal with particular problems. Their effect has been to give a measure of protection for trade union activities against the application of common law doctrines and legal judgments antagonistic to the collective struggle of workers within capitalist society. This protection has enabled the unions to work effectively in many sections of industry. On the other hand, millions of workers employed in jobs where it is more difficult to organise effectively or where there is little tradition of trade unionism and collective bargaining are still subject to various pressures from employers to keep them out of the unions; some of these are sharp and direct.

Far too often in this connection, middle-class opinion has a false picture of trade union power. It imagines that unions abuse the civil liberties of men and women by compelling them to act in a manner contrary to their natural inclinations. This has very little relationship to the truth. The effectiveness of trade union action depends more than anything else on a combination of decisive and committed leadership and rank and file support.

The right of association and collective bargaining, which all workers ought to possess, is frequently infringed by the hostility of employers. This hostility can make itself apparent in a thousand and one different ways ranging from the outright victimisation of a representative to subtle hints to active and talented trade unionists that they are making themselves "ineligible" for promotion.

Employers sometimes also seek to evade union claims by parallel and competing offers of concessions.

The right of all workers to join a union and to participate in trade union activities ought to be protected *in a positive way*. It is not sufficient to say, as in effect is said in British law, that it is not unlawful to organise for trade union purposes. In Britain it is equally not unlawful for an employer to seek to prevent—or destroy—trade union organisation.

Why not the ILO Conventions?

The constitution of the International Labour Organisation—a specialised agency of the United Nations, representing governments, employers and workers in many countries—contains a formal mandate to safeguard freedom of association. The preamble to the constitution of the ILO asserts that the recognition of the principle of the freedom of association is one of the means of improving the conditions of the workers and of ensuring peace. This right of association has also been endorsed by the General Assembly of the United Nations. In 1947 the Assembly passed a resolution which contained the following two clauses:

> Considers that the inalienable right of trade union freedom of association is, as well as other social safeguards, essential to the improvement of the standard of living of workers and to their economic well-being;
> Declares that it endorses the principles proclaimed by the International Labour Conference in respect of trade union rights as well as the principles the importance of which to labour has already been recognised and which are mentioned in the Constitution of the International Labour Organisation and in the Declaration of Philadelphia. . . .

The most explicit international instruments providing protection for the right to organise and the right to bargain collectively are provided by two ILO Conventions, namely the Freedom of Association and Protection of the Right to Organise Convention, 1948 (No. 87) and the Right to Organise and Collective Bargaining Convention, 1949 (No. 98). The first of these conventions defines certain fundamental principles which are intended to enable workers and employers to exercise their right to organise without interference from the State or other public authorities. The second is designed to protect the right to organise against the hostile actions of employers. It also calls for measures to be taken, where necessary, to encourage and promote collective bargaining. These two conventions are of such vital importance that they deserve close consideration. The United Kingdom has ratified both conventions but has not given affirmative legal effect to their main requirements. This is, perhaps, not very surprising. The settled policy of successive governments has been to contemplate action when median performance surpasses the minima demanded by convention.

The 1948 Convention lays down the following main principles:

First principle: Workers and employers, without distinction whatsoever, shall have the right to establish and, subject only to the rules of the organisation concerned, to join organisations of their own choosing without previous authorisation. The words "without distinction whatsoever" are intended to emphasise that the right to organise must be enjoyed by all without discrimination, irrespective of nationality, religion, sex, political opinion or occupation. The only restriction allowed is in relation to the armed forces and the police. Article 9 of the Convention says that the extent to which the guarantees which it provides shall apply to the armed forces and the police shall be determined by national laws or regulations.

The words "without previous authorisation" are intended to proclaim that the workers' right to organise is a *fundamental* social right and is not one for which he needs the permission of his employer or anyone else. Moreover it is a right which must be respected by the State.

Second principle: Workers' and employers' organisations shall enjoy independence to draw up their own rules, to formulate their own policies and to elect their own representatives. The State must not assume administrative powers to interfere with their independence.

Third principle: Workers' and employers' organisations shall have the right to establish and to join federations of similar organisations and to affiliate with international organisations of workers and employers.

The Convention says that in exercising their rights workers and employers and their organisations shall respect the law of the land. The law of the land, however, must not be such as to impair the guarantees provided for in the Convention.

The 1949 Convention goes beyond a declaration of principles. To put it another way: the 1948 Convention *affirms* certain social rights; the 1949 Convention seeks to *protect* the exercise of these rights against discrimination from others. It declares that workers are entitled to enjoy adequate protection in their employment against acts of anti-union discrimination. Such protection, it adds, shall apply more particularly against acts calculated to make the employment of a worker subject to the condition that he shall not join a union or shall relinquish trade union membership; or cause the dismissal or prejudice the position or prospects of a worker because of trade union membership or because of union activities outside working hours or, with the consent of the employer, within working hours.

The 1949 Convention also states that workers' and employers' organisations shall enjoy adequate protection against interference by each other in their establishment, functioning or administration. Actions designed to promote the establishment of workers' organisations under the domination of employers are deemed to constitute acts of interference for the purpose of the Convention.

The Convention further states that, where necessary, machinery shall be set up for the purpose of ensuring that the right to organise is respected. It also calls for the establishment, where necessary, of measures to encourage and promote the full development and utilisation of machinery of collective bargaining.

Neither the 1948 nor the 1949 Convention contains anything to protect the so called right "not to organise". Amendments designed to give such protection were submitted but were defeated. There are strong arguments against giving any kind of legal protection to this spurious right "not to organise". The refusal of a worker to join a union affects not only his own interests but also the interests of all who work with him. He can be—and so often is—exploited by the employer to the ultimate detriment of everyone else.

If a non-unionist claims the right "not to organise" (although he takes the benefits) then others who work with him and who are trade unionists can claim the right not to work with someone whose conduct threatens their own interests. This problem cannot be settled by regarding human rights in isolation from the social circumstances in which they are exercised. If any sense of social reality is to be maintained the right of workers to organise in trade unions cannot be equated with a claim to be permitted "not to organise".

It is the experience of trade unions that nearly all of those who refuse to join a union in a workshop or office where the great majority are union members do so not from high principle but from extremely selfish motives. They boast of their indifference to the welfare of others and claim that they get the benefits of collective agreements without paying union dues. This kind of selfishness inflames feeling among the majority who accept the responsibility to maintain the machinery of collective bargaining by contributing to union funds. It is unreasonable to expect trade unionists to do nothing about such individuals. They have every right to say that they are not prepared to work with them.

There is, on the other hand, among non-unionists in strongly organised workplaces an extremely tiny majority who, because of their religious views, refuse to join organisations which include "non-believers". In such cases it is preferable for all concerned to provide a means of conscientious objection. Two conditions, however, need to be satisfied. The first is that the objector should satisfy those with whom he works that his religious scruples about joining an organisation which includes "non-believers" are sincerely held and do not apply only to trade unionism. Secondly, the conscientious objector should be expected to pay the equivalent of the union subscription to a mutually agreed charity or benevolent fund. He will not then be subject to the jibe that his conscientious objection to trade union membership puts him at a financial advantage over others with whom he works.

Article 11 of the 1948 Convention stipulates that member States which ratify it shall "take all necessary and appropriate measures to ensure that workers and employers may exercise freely the right to organise". A number of countries, though not Britain, protect the right to organise by law and make it an offence for anyone to infringe it. The best example is probably that provided by Sweden.

A Swedish Law which seems to Work

In 1936 in Sweden a Right of Association and Collective Bargaining Act was passed. This gave statutory form to rights which were already enjoyed by many Swedish workers but which rested on the strength of trade union organisation. The right of association could also be inferred from provisions of the Swedish constitution and from previous court decisions.

The 1936 Act states that the "right of association" for employers and employees shall mean:

(1) The right to belong to an association, the duty of which according to its rules is to defend the interests of employees/employers in connection with conditions of employment and relations with employers/employees in general.
(2) The right to exercise their rights as members of an association.
(3) The right to work on behalf of an association.
(4) The right to work for the formation of an association.

The Act does not protect the so-called right "not to associate". According to the book *Collective Bargaining in Sweden* by T. L. Johnston, three reasons were given for confining protection to the "right to associate". In the first place it was felt that legislation on such a far reaching issue as the "right not to associate" could not be confined to the labour market. Secondly, it was felt that compulsion to organise is an internal matter for workers and employers. The Act does not deal with the internal affairs of unions or employers' organisations but provides for each side to be able to exercise the right of combination. Thirdly, it was felt that the right to associate should be regulated only to the extent necessary to guarantee the right of negotiation.

When an ILO mission went to Sweden in 1960 they found that, "The high degree of organisation achieved in practice, and which has the support of both sides, tends to make the question of the closed shop one of academic interest only". They observed, nevertheless, that closed shop agreements covering a small number of workers are sometimes concluded with unorganised employers whose influence, in the opinion of the unions, may deter the workers from applying for union membership. A closed shop clause in a collective agreement is regarded as being compatible with the "right of association". On the other hand a closed shop clause does not legally prevent a worker from choosing the union to which he wants to belong. The Swedish courts have taken the view that the right of association is infringed when a worker is dismissed or threatened with dismissal for refusing to join the union with which the employer has concluded an agreement.

Swedish experience appears in this respect to confirm one of the conclusions reached by Dr. McCarthy in his study *The Closed Shop in Britain*. He felt that the closed shop was, in general terms, justifiable because in certain circumstances it enabled the unions to overcome weaknesses which would otherwise be exploited by employers. Where there is little danger of such exploitation there was usually no strong demand for the closed shop.

Special provision is made in Swedish law in applying the "right of association" to foremen. The law provides that it is permissible—though not obligatory—to include in a collective agreement or a personal contract of employment a clause forbidding foremen to belong to "an association the aim of which is to defend the interests of the employees subordinate to him . . . ". Other than this restriction, however, the "right of association" is enjoyed by foremen as by other workers in Sweden—and they have established a strong and vigorous union.

The Swedish 1936 Act also provides a positive legal "right of negotiation". This means, according to the Act, "the right to institute negotiations respecting the adjustment of conditions of employment and respecting the relations between employers and employees in general". The right applies both to unions and to employers or employers' organisations. The "right of negotiation" conferred upon either side imposes on the other side an obligation to enter into negotiations.

An oft-used argument against the introduction of positive legal rights of association and negotiation is that it might encourage the formation of splinter organisations. Swedish experience does not give any support to this argument. Indeed, the Swedish trade union movement has a much more regular pattern of organisation than the British trade union movement. There are fewer unions and most of the manual workers are in vertical, industrial organisations. The white collar workers are powerfully organised in distinctive unions of the salariat with their own union centre (TCO).

It is important to note that Swedish law on the right of association and negotiation is so framed that it discourages rather than encourages splinter organisations. In industrial disputes there, the representative character of a trade union carries weight when assistance is sought from the Swedish equivalent of the British conciliation service. A trade union may register with the Social Welfare Board (a government agency concerned with social welfare problems and the labour mediation service) providing that it submits a copy of its rules, a list of the persons who are members of its governing body and a copy of the minutes of a meeting approving the rules and the election of the governing body. If the union then seeks assistance in a dispute—for example to establish the right of negotiation with an employer—the Social Welfare Board may refuse to appoint an official mediator if (a) the union represents less than half the workers affected by the dispute, or (b) the union has less than 300 members, or (c) the membership of the union is not open to all persons in the category or categories whose interests the union claims to defend.

The practical effect of these provisions is to discourage the formation of breakaway or splinter organisations.

Swedish law on the right to organise and bargain collectively is far in advance of any legislation adopted by Britain. It forms part of a framework of law on industrial relations which, however, it would be neither possible nor desirable to bring in identical form to Britain. In Sweden, as in Britain, there is a strong tradition against government interference in wage bargaining but there is stronger legislative provision for conciliation. Collective agreements are wider in scope and the rights of unions and of workers are generally more firmly based than in Britain. A clear distinction is made between disputes about the terms of existing agreements and disputes which arise when new agreements are being negotiated. As the TUC pointed out in their booklet *Sweden—Its Unions and Industrial Relations*: "Collective agreements are binding in law both on the parties and on their members, and strikes and lockouts during the life of an agreement are in general illegal and can and do attract damages."

It would not be desirable to introduce this feature into Britain.

Laws Against Anti-union Discrimination

A number of countries protect the right to organise by prohibiting any contract of employment whereby one of the parties undertakes not to become or to remain a member of an occupational association. According to the ILO manual *Freedom of Association*, contracts of this kind are null and void in Canada, Cuba, Egypt, Finland, Haiti, the Netherlands, Turkey, the United States, Uruguay and a number of other countries.

Some countries also outlaw certain forms of anti-union discrimination, including:

> The recruitment of a worker only on condition that he does not join a union or leaves the union to which he already belongs.

Discrimination against a worker during his employment because of his union membership or activities.

The dismissal of, or threat to dismiss, a worker because of his union membership or activities.

The use of pressure, intimidation or coercion calculated to restrict, either directly or indirectly, a worker's freedom of association.

The manual *Freedom of Association* states that legislation of this type exists in Argentina, Australia, Belgium, Brazil, Bolivia, Canada, Colombia, Costa Rica, Egypt, Finland, Japan, Mexico, Nicaragua, the Philippines, the United States, Uruguay, Venezuela and a few other countries.

A New Law for Britain?

The right to organise and to bargain collectively ought to be protected *positively* by British law. At present these affirmative legal rights do not exist, even though many lawyers and other commentators often speak of the legal position of the unions as though, in Britain, the unions enjoyed special privileges. This habit of speech arises really from the manner in which the legal position of the unions has evolved, and it betrays also an unspoken assumption that it is a "privilege" for workers to have the right to combine and to use their collective strength for protective trade purposes. Professor K. W. Wedderburn in an article in the October 1964 issue of *Federation News*, the journal of the General Federation of Trade Unions, put it this way:

> Trade unions are often accused of having legal "privileges". Except for the unimportant area of union immunity to take actions outside trade union disputes, this accusation is quite unfounded. But the legal *form* of our labour law gives rise to the impression. As we saw, the liberty of action which is absolutely necessary for trade union activity and modern collective negotiation has been provided by "immunities" or "privileges" in trade disputes for union officials and workers, to protect them from judge-made liabilities which would have made modern collective bargaining impossible. What appear as rights in other systems of law (e.g. a "right to strike") appear in our system as liberties protected by these "immunities".

If certain basic trade union rights were to be protected by law it would still be desirable, as far as possible, to keep disputed issues out of the normal courts. Fortunately this could be achieved by utilising institutions and methods developed and shaped by past British practice. The law ought to affirm that all employees and employers have a right to organise to protect and further their interests. It should be unlawful for anyone to seek to interfere with this right or to interfere with the right of another person to participate in the activities of a trade union or employers' organisation of which he is a member.

The observance of the law could be monitored by providing that complaints that the right to organise was not being observed or that there was interference with the right to organise should be submitted in the first instance to the party against whom the complaint was made. If the complaint was not resolved it could then be submitted to whatever joint machinery, if any, might exist in the section of industry concerned. If it was still unresolved the assistance of the conciliation service of the Ministry of Labour could then be sought. If this still proved unsuccessful the complaint could then be submitted to the Industrial Court. The Industrial Court ought to have discretionary powers as to how such a complaint should be heard and in what form its recommendations or, if necessary, an award should be made. The Court could, for example, "inquire and report" on the substance of the complaint, or alternatively, it could conciliate or mediate between the parties. If necessary, in order to resolve the complaint, it should have the power to award that the "right to organise" be observed. This right would then become an implied term of the contract and, if necessary, could be enforced in a normal court of law. The emphasis of this whole process, however, would be such that the normal courts would not be involved except on rare occasions. The power to make complaints would rest with representative organisations.

The right of workers to participate in trade union activities, without interference from their employer, would need also to be defined. It should cover the following:

The right to nominate, to elect and to be elected as a workplace trade union representative.

The right to circulate at the place of employment official notices and literature distributed by the union of which the workpeople are members. This should include the right to display official union notices on a union notice board located within the premises of the workplace.

The right of officially appointed representatives to collect union subscriptions at the workplace at intervals not more frequently than once a week. The arrangements should be made in co-operation with the management to suit the convenience of all concerned and to have regard to the requirements of the job.

The right of all workers to meet for official trade union purposes at reasonable intervals in their own time in a suitable room or shop (e.g. the canteen) at the place of employment.

These rights could be defined in general terms by regulations under a Right to Organise Act. It should, however, be left to the employers and unions, with the assistance of the conciliation service of the Ministry of Labour and, if necessary, the Industrial Court, to build up by experience an understanding of the practical application of these rights.* It would be helpful, in the absence of other legislation, if the Fair Wages Resolution were strengthened to provide for the observance of specified trade union rights.

For the observance of the right to negotiate a similar procedure for dealing with complaints should be observed as in relation to the right to organise. Safeguards would, however, have to be provided to discourage breakaway and splinter organisations. This ought not to be insurmountable. Something might be adopted on the Swedish pattern. Thus the Industrial Court would not be required to consider complaints that the "right to negotiate" was not being observed if the complaint was submitted by an

* See also the constructive suggestions in the Labour Party booklet, *Industrial Democracy*, June 1967.

organisation which was not representative of a substantial number of the workers concerned or if satisfactory collective bargaining arrangements already existed. It would probably be wiser
not to define these matters too closely, but to leave their interpretation to the discretion of the parties concerned and the Industrial
Court.

In some countries when questions of trade union recognition
arise, notably the USA, it is customary to take a ballot among
the workers concerned to ascertain their wishes. It is then possible
for the workers to vote for or against trade union recognition and,
if necessary, to choose between competing unions. Suggestions
for such a procedure in Britain have been very rarely made. Undoubtedly the procedure would have disadvantages. But the
advantages of a balloting system would be that a means would be
provided for workers to express their view. It might also have the
effect of eliminating overlapping membership in a number of
occupations. A right of trade union recognition ought not to be
interpreted as granting negotiating rights to every union claiming
a mere handful of members among a group of workers of the
same occupation who, in the majority, are members of another
union. A balloting system might also encourage unions to be
responsive to the wishes of members.

The disadvantages of a balloting system are that in many
industries and services—given the present trade union structure—
it would not be easy to define the various bargaining units for
voting purposes. In the engineering industry, for example, the
lines of demarcation and the areas of overlap between different
unions vary from one factory to another. Balloting might also
encourage one union to "raid" the membership of another union
if a ballot were about to be held. It could thus make for instability.
If there were to be ballots for recognition in certain circumstances
it might also be argued that provision should be made, in response
to requests, for ballots for the ending of recognition. Workers
might be subject to a burst of hostile propaganda and influenced
to vote against continued recognition. They might also be influenced by temporary considerations.

Clearly, in the light of the history of industrial relations in Britain there is no likelihood of a widespread system of balloting for trade union recognition being introduced. Nevertheless it is a method which occasionally might be suitable in circumstances decided by an Industrial Court consisting of experienced persons.

The role of the Industrial Court in helping to ensure that the right to organise and the right to negotiate was observed in British industry and commerce would be a vital one. Persons appointed to the Industrial Court should continue to be chosen from among men and women with wide experience in industrial relations. Only a minority should be lawyers. It would, of course, probably be necessary to enlarge the membership of the Court so that it could sit, if necessary, in panels to deal with cases brought before it. Because the members of the Court are experienced in industrial relations they could be expected to use their influence to discourage breakaway and splinter organisations on both sides of industry.

The introduction by law of a positive right to bargain collectively does not imply that negotiating procedure agreements between employers and unions should be enforceable in the courts or that breaches of procedure should provide grounds for legal action. Agreements on procedure should continue to be regarded —as they have generally been regarded in the past—as voluntary instruments. All that the law should seek to uphold is that the right to negotiate exists; not whether a particular procedure has been observed. The question as to whether procedure has been observed or broken may very well be an issue on which the Industrial Court—if it reaches that level—may wish to pronounce, but it should not give grounds for legal action unless the Court awards that the right to bargain collectively has not been observed. An award that such a right must be observed would be legally enforceable. Providing that an employer agreed to meet the union concerned and to enter into negotiations in good faith he would discharge his legal obligation. It would not be the function of the courts to compel the observance of a particular procedure or even to insist that agreement should be reached. If agreement could not be reached by negotiation the union could seek either to enforce its claim by strike or other dispute action or submit it to an arbitration tribunal. Such a tribunal could be constituted independently on the lines of the former Industrial Disputes Tribunal* or could be the Industrial Court itself. It would be essential that, as with the former Industrial Disputes Tribunal, cases could be referred for arbitration by the Ministry of Labour without such a step first requiring the consent of the employer against whom the claim is being made.

The introduction of new law affirmatively to protect the right to organise and to bargain collectively would not only protect essential social rights, but it would also give a much needed stimulus to trade union organisation, particularly among white collar workers. Millions of additional workers could be recruited into the trade unions if the fear and intimidation which exists in so many fields of employment were removed. The introduction of new law would not bring to an end the hostility of many employers towards trade unionism, but at least it would make them much more hesitant about carrying their disapproval to the point where they actively discouraged or tried to disrupt trade union organisation among their employees.

* The Terms and Conditions of Employment Act, 1959, was passed by Parliament shortly after the winding up of the Industrial Disputes Tribunal. This Tribunal was established under the Industrial Disputes Order, 1951. It continued in a modified form the National Arbitration Tribunal established during the Second World War. The Order was revoked in 1958 and the Tribunal came to an end early in 1959. The Industrial Disputes Order, 1951, provided for compulsory arbitration only in a restricted sense. It did not prohibit strikes or lockouts. Employers or unions could if they so wished—providing that the normal machinery of negotiation was exhausted—take a dispute to the Minister of Labour for reference to the Tribunal without having to secure the consent of the other party. The dispute would not be referred to the Tribunal if a strike or lockout took place with a view to enforcing the claim. Any award of the Tribunal was legally enforceable because it became part of the contract of employment of those covered by it. The Tribunal was abolished largely on the insistence of the employers. It had always been accepted that the Tribunal would continue in existence only so long as it was supported by the principal employers' and workers' organisations. The TUC have subsequently urged that something similar to the Industrial Disputes Tribunal should be restored.

Whether Britain adopts the Swedish method or some other method of protecting the right to organise and to bargain collectively, one thing is clear: the present arrangements are unfairly tilted against the unions.

CHAPTER 4

Complaints under ILO conventions— and the case of the FSMBS

IN SPITE of many examples of employer resistance to unionisation there have been only two disputes in recent years in Britain in which formal complaints have been made that ILO conventions on the right to organise and the right to bargain collectively have been violated. Neither of these complaints, however, concerned straightforward cases of non-recognition, and one involved a small and clearly unrepresentative organisation in conflict with all the other unions in the field in which it sought to establish itsels.

This organisation was the Aeronautical Engineers' Association which lodged a complaint with the ILO in 1954. This Association organised a handful of engineers employed by the nationalised civil airways corporations. Although a registered trade union it was not affiliated to the TUC and it was constantly skirmishing with the other airline unions. It alleged that its members were debarred from employment in a number of departments where other unions, recognised by the airways corporations, had established 100 per cent membership. It was further alleged that members of the AEA were not only denied the opportunity to work in certain shops but were also passed over for promotion because of their membership of the Association. This, the AEA argued, was contrary to the rights of employees guaranteed by ILO Convention.

The complaints made by the AEA were considered by the ILO Committee on Freedom of Association. The Committee did not find in favour of the AEA. They acknowledged that membership of the recognised unions carried with it a number of advantages and that membership of the AEA had a number of disadvantages from the point of view of the worker's employment.

Nevertheless, it was their view, based on previous declarations of the ILO, that

> the managements in this case are acting in accordance with the union security arrangements agreed upon between the parties and the operation of which may, in effect, cause a worker "to withdraw from a union to which he belongs" but not "to relinquish trade union membership" and may cause a worker to suffer certain prejudices in his employment "by reason of his membership in a union" but not "by reason of union membership".

The Committee, in fact, upheld the existing highly developed bargaining system which sprang from the Civil Aviation Act of 1946.

The ILO Committee also stated that the AEA had failed to establish their complaint that the refusal of the employers to recognise them as a bargaining agent constituted an infringement of trade union rights. They pointed out that the ILO Convention did not place a duty on a government to enforce bargaining by compulsory means with a *given* organisation. Regard had to be paid in this connection to the interpretation of the conventions by the ILO in the light of union security arrangements. In other words, the maintenance of a 100 per cent union shop, by agreement with the employer, does not constitute a violation of the rights of employees who are not members of the union which is party to the agreement. The decision was a sensible one; the AEA was supported by a small minority mainly for historical reasons arising out of past union quarrels.

Bank Employees

A much more disquieting case and one more typical of the kind of problem often faced by white-collar unions in Britain concerned the right of bank workers to organise and to take part in collective bargaining in four main British banks. The National Union of

Bank Employees complained that it was being prevented from exercising its proper functions as a trade union because of the existence of staff associations recognised by the managements in the District, Martins, National Provincial and Yorkshire banks. These staff associations, it was said, were being supported by the banking employers and therefore a state of affairs existed in breach of the ILO Convention on the right to organise and to bargain which had been ratified by the United Kingdom. The NUBE submitted evidence to illustrate the determination of the four banks to sustain and support their respective staff associations to the exclusion and detriment of the NUBE. The banks claimed, on the other hand, that the staff associations were free and independent of their influence.

The complaint was submitted by the National Union of Bank Employees in 1962 to the Committee on Freedom of Association of the ILO. The Minister of Labour then decided to appoint Lord Cameron to inquire into the complaint and to report. In his report Lord Cameron stated that having heard the evidence he had reached the conclusion that "the complaint was not drafted with a sense of responsibility commensurate with the gravity of the charges which it preferred". He found no evidence that the four banks interfered with their staff associations and he did not consider that the facilities, which they admittedly received from the banks, brought them under the domination or control of the employers. Lord Cameron said that in his view the real basis of the charge of hostility which the union made against the banks was that they continued to recognise their own staff associations but refused to recognise the NUBE. NUBE, of course, continued to be suspicious of these internal arrangements, probably echoing Sir Walter Raleigh's view: "If she seem not chaste to me, what care I how chaste she be?"

Lord Cameron did not confine his report to an examination of the complaint of the NUBE as, sensibly, there were other issues of interlocking importance. He went on to make suggestions to improve the relationship between the banks and the NUBE and advocated that the realities of the situation should lead responsibly minded men, both in the NUBE and in the staff associations, to recognise that both bodies were representative organisations. He proposed that an examination should be made with the help of the Ministry of Labour of the methods by which the NUBE could make representations on behalf of their members in the four banks named in the complaint. Consideration might then be given to the possibility of reaching an agreement on national matters effecting the banking industry, such as base scales, and upon machinery for joint consultation. Lord Cameron envisaged that the NUBE and certain staff associations would co-operate to form the employees' side of the machinery which he had suggested. A group or committee of banks would form the employers' side.

Lord Cameron said that his suggestion for the setting-up of such joint machinery was not confined to the District, Martins, the National Provincial and Yorkshire banks. He hoped that it would extend over a wider field and would include other banks.

If new law had been introduced into Britain, to protect affirmatively the right to organise and the right to bargain collectively, and if the law had been administered by the Industrial Court on the lines advocated in the preceding chapter, it is interesting to speculate what might have been the outcome of the two complaints outlined in this appendix. Almost certainly the complaint of the AEA would have failed. It would have failed on the grounds outlined in the findings of the ILO Committee on Freedom of Association.

The complaint of the NUBE, however, would have led, with almost equal certainty, to recognition of the union by the banks. This recognition *might* have been accorded solely to the NUBE or jointly with certain staff associations as suggested by Lord Cameron. It is inconceivable, given a statutory right to bargain collectively, that the wishes of tens of thousands of bank employees organised within the NUBE would continue to be frustrated.

NUBE submitted its complaint in 1962. It took 19 months after the Cameron Report for a joint working party to be set up (representing the union, nine clearing banks and staff associations) and even this was not entirely representative because at the time the Midland Bank and the National Provincial Bank (together with their staff associations) declined to take part in the talks. Eventually when the working party produced its report the National Provincial Bank and its staff associations agreed to sign it. The working party reached agreement for three constitutions for a joint negotiating council, a Federation of Bank Employers and a Banking Staff Council. In July 1967, however, it was announced that the plan for the establishment of national negotiating machinery had collapsed because of inadequate support from the staff associations. The banks concluded that effective machinery could not therefore be established "at this stage".

The whole process must have been extremely frustrating to the NUBE. After 5 years, following their complaint about recognition, they are still denied effective collective bargaining. This is an injustice. There must be faster, more decisive procedures for dealing with such situations.

Anti-union organisations

One immediate effect of new legislation to protect the right to organise and to bargain collectively would be to outlaw professional anti-union organisations. The absence of any legislation to protect the right to organise and to bargain collectively has left employers completely free to indulge in all kinds of anti-union activity in complete contravention of ILO conventions. Most non-manual workers' unions have had to contend with house and staff associations directly supported by employers with the object of frustrating the growth of genuine trade unionism amongst their staff.

A particularly blatant type of employer-sponsored organisation is the Foreman and Staff Mutual Benefit Society which is openly and arrogantly ranged against bona-fide union organisation. This Society was established in 1899 as a friendly society ostensibly to provide sick benefits and pensions for its members. In fact, it was meant as a dyke against unionism. It is worth some study. The Society's constitution provides for two classes of members:

(a) *Contributory members:*
Firms, companies, corporations and other employers approved by the Executive Council of the Society.

(b) *Ordinary members:*
Foremen, under-foremen and all employees holding positions of trust or employed on the management, technical, office or commercial staff at the age of 21 or over. Such people are eligible to join provided they are proposed by the contributory member by whom they are employed. The entrance fee of 10s. is payable, one half by the contributory member proposing the ordinary member, and one half by the ordinary member himself.

Since its inception, the Society has had a rule (rule 7) stipulating that it is not possible to belong both to the Society and to a trade union. Originally, rule 7 read as follows:

Members of a trade union, either registered or unregistered, shall not be eligible as ordinary members of the Society, and if any ordinary member becomes a member of a trade union, either registered or unregistered, he shall thereupon cease to be a member of this Society.

During the last decade, however, increasing numbers of non-manual staff have become attracted to trade unionism. In 1962 in face of a threatened court action, the Foremen and Staff Mutual Benefit Society was forced to pay the surrender value of his contributions to a member who had also joined ASSET. It must then have been decided that the anti-union provisions in its rules were not strong enough to meet the situation and in 1963, on the recommendation of the Executive Council of the Society, the following new rules were approved:

Rule 7

An ordinary member who at the date of his admission to the Society is a member of a trade union, registered or unregistered, shall forthwith resign from such trade union. If he fails to do so he shall immediately resign from the Society. An ordinary member who, after admission to the Society, joins any such trade union shall immediately resign from the Society. An ordinary member who fails to resign immediately from the Society in terms of this Rule shall cease to have any claim on the funds of the Society either by way of benefits or return of contributions or premiums or any part thereof or otherwise, shall be liable to make good to

the Society any funds improperly received or retained by him and shall
be liable to expulsion under Rule 11.

Rule 11

Any ordinary member who shall have obtained admission to the Society
by misrepresentation, or who shall have made any mis-statement as to his
age or condition of health, or who shall fail to comply with the provisions
of Rule 7, or who shall continue to be a member of or shall obtain any
benefit from the Society under false pretences, or whose conduct is such
as to be in the opinion of the Executive Council injurious to the interests
of the Society may, subject to Rule 100, be expelled by a resolution of the
Executive Council, provided such resolution is carried by not less than
two-thirds of those present at the meeting. Such ordinary member shall
thereupon cease to have any claim on the funds of the Society, either by
way of benefits or return of contributions or premiums or any part thereof
or otherwise, and he shall also be liable to make good to the Society any
funds improperly received or retained by him. The Executive Council
shall have power, but shall not be bound, to pay any member or the
dependants of any member who has ceased to have any claim on the
funds of the Society in terms of Rule 7, or who has been expelled in terms
of this Rule, a sum not exceeding the cash surrender value of his forfeited
benefits.

According to the last available annual report, the membership
comprises 2605 contributory members (firms) and 60,000 ordinary members (employees). Among the firms which are known to
have been contributory members are some of the largest in the
country. They include:

British Motor Corporation Limited
Smiths Industries Limited
Howell & Company (Subsidiary of Tube Investments)
    Limited
Cammel Laird & Company Limited
John I. Thorneycroft & Company Limited
Vickers Armstrong Limited
General Electric Company Limited
Vauxhall Motors Limited
English Steel Corporation Limited
Rolls-Royce Limited
Stothert & Pitt Limited
Hawker Siddeley Group Limited

Rootes Group Limited
English Electric Limited

In fact many thousands of F & SMBS members have joined ASSET and applied for the surrender value of their contributions or—where they joined the anti-union body under duress—have simply kept on their F & SMBS membership as well. Some employers pay treble the employees' contributions and all the employers' payments are lost to the man who withdraws for ethical reasons. This can mean a substantial sum if he has been a member for a long period and this, of course, is a disincentive to joining a union if he is, say, older than 55 years and contemplating retirement.

In many cases the local representative of the F & SMBS is a member of the personnel management, and, when ASSET has freshly organised a factory great pressure is put upon the new members to leave the union. Representatives of the F & SMBS have been given facilities to interview staff on the firm's premises.

The weekly contribution is a joint one, payable by the employer and employee. The share of each party is not specified, but a normal arrangement appears to be a contribution of 5s. per week per ordinary member, half being paid by the employee and the other by the employer. However, as already indicated, there is an increasing tendency on the part of employers to multiply their share in order to offset the attractions of trade union membership. In some cases the employer pays the employees' contributions as well.

The benefits of the F & SMBS are ostensibly friendly society insurance benefits. But it is clear that the main reason for the continued support given to the Society by many large firms is its anti-union rule. Many firms make it known to people seeking promotion that it is expected of them that they will join the F & SMBS on promotion. When they do so, of course, they have to relinquish trade union membership. Once promoted, they are understandably reluctant to join a trade union because they fear they may lose the F & SMBS benefits for which they have contributed, as well as incurring the positive displeasure of their employer. The F & SMBS is thus an instrument for the taming of the staff, while making them pay for it at the same time.

It is clear that the existence of the F & SMBS in its present form offends against the spirit and intention of ILO conventions which have been ratified by Britain. The F & SMBS is an outrageous social anachronism. Its continued existence mocks the British Government's ratification of Convention 87 of the ILO which protects the right of workers to join organisations of their own choice. Article 11 of Convention 87 reads as follows. "Each member of the International Labour Organisation for which this Convention is in force undertakes to take all necessary and appropriate measures to ensure that workers and employers may freely exercise the right to organise."

It also derides articles 1 and 2 of Convention 98 which was drafted to protect workers against acts of anti-trade union discrimination. These declared:

Article 1

(1) Workers shall enjoy adequate protection against acts of anti-union discrimination in respect of their employment.

(2) Such protection shall apply more particularly in respect of acts calculated to:

(a) make the employment of a worker subject to the condition that he shall not join a union or shall relinquish trade union membership;
(b) cause the dismissal of or otherwise prejudice a worker by reason of union membership or because of participation in union activities outside working hours or, with the consent of the employer, within working hours.

Article 2

(1) Workers' and employers' organisations shall enjoy adequate protection against any acts of interference by each other or each other's agents or members in their establishment, functioning or administration.

(2) In particular, acts which are designed to promote the establishment of workers' organisations under the domination of employers or employers' organisations, or to support workers' organisations by financial or other means, with the object of placing such organisations under the control of employers or employers' organisations, shall be deemed to constitute acts of interference within the meaning of this Article.

Unfortunately, British practice has been to *avoid* legislation which would put teeth into admirable conventions to which parliamentary lip service has been paid.

There have been a number of attempts by MPs to deal with the F & SMBS by legislation: the most recent of these was the introduction of the Friendly Societies (Membership of Trade Unions) Bill by Mr. John Diamond, MP, in June 1964. The object of the Bill was to invalidate the rules of any friendly society discriminating against membership of trade unions. The Bill failed to make progress at that time, but it would have been one effective way of dealing with this anti-trade union organisation.

The Labour Party is on record as favouring legislation to exorcise the offending rule but ASSET has been informed that action must await the report of the Royal Commission on Trade Unions and Employers' Associations. There can be no possible objection to the F & SMBS continuing as a friendly society, once its anti-trade union bias has been removed. Of course, whether employers would continue to support it financially in such circumstances is open to some doubt: in our opinion its *raison d'être* is its anti-trade union role, and without this provision in its rules it would fall into desuetude. On the other hand, if legislation were introduced to give positive effect to ILO Conventions 87 and 98, the F & SMBS would be presented with the alternative either of amending its rules itself to remove the anti-trade union provisions or else of going out of existence altogether. There would thus be no need for special legislation of the type envisaged by Mr. Diamond in his 1964 Bill.

The American View

The American National Labour Relations Board* would certainly have classified employer support for such a body as an

---

* The National Labour Relations Board was established by the National Labour Relations Act, 1935. Among other functions it has the task of helping to ensure that the right to organise and to bargain collectively is properly observed in the USA.

unfair labour practice. In the USA such intimidatory tactics are impermissible. Companies are even forbidden to appeal to union members over the heads of the union representatives. A celebrated complaint by the International Union of Electrical Workers against the General Electric Company was reported thus by the *New York Times* (17 December, 1964).

> The National Labour Relations Board handed down a decision today that could ban an employer from expressing his views to his workers while bargaining with their union.
> The Board by a 4–1 vote ruled that the General Electric Company failed to bargain in good faith with the International Union of Electrical Workers in contract negotiations in 1960.
> One of the major findings was that the company's effort to present its views through plant newspapers, press releases and radio announcements was part of a campaign to undermine the union. . . .

The Board accused General Electric of trying to discredit the union with "an intensive" communications programme addressed to workers. The NLRB said an employer is not permitted to "bargain directly or indirectly with the employees", but must deal directly with their union.

"It is inconsistent with this obligation for an employer to mount a campaign, as (G.E.) did, both before and during negotiations, for the purpose of disparaging and discrediting the statutory representative in the eyes of its employee constituents", the Board said in its ruling. It said such tactics sought "to persuade the employees to exert pressure on the representative to submit to the will of the employer, and to create the impression that the employer rather than the union is the true protector of the employee's interests".

We need to be unblinkered about what is going on in the world. After all, if a complaint to the ILO were upheld trade union recognition in Britain would *still* depend on the goodwill and agreement of the employer. He could not be compelled to engage in collective bargaining with a union representing his workpeople. This is not a satisfactory way to uphold fundamental social rights.

CHAPTER 5

Security of employment—and the employee's inadequate protection against arbitrary dismissal

THE traditional—and effete—British view on the function of the law in relation to the dismissal of workers from employment is that it should be limited to insisting upon a proper period of notice. In the past this period of notice for many workers was only one hour. Later it was extended by collective agreements between employers and trade unions. "Guaranteed week" agreements concluded in the last 25 years have given to substantial numbers of industrial workers the right to a period of notice, on termination of employment, of not less than one week.

More recently still, the Contracts of Employment Act, 1963, has linked notice with service and extended the minimum period of notice for workers with more than a given length of employment. Workers with more than 6 months' service are now entitled to a minimum period of notice of one week. Workers with more than 2 years' service, but with less than 5 years' service, get a minimum period of notice of a fortnight, and workers with more than 5 years' service with their employer are entitled to one month. The Act requires an employee to give his employer at least one week's notice if he has been with him continuously for 26 weeks or more. This does not increase with longer service.

Philosophy of Abstention

The view that the responsibility of the law in relation to the dismissal of a worker should be limited to insisting on a minimum period of notice is part of a wider concept that little, if anything, ought to be done to interfere with the free operation of the industrial system. It also partly reflects trade union inertia. It is argued that to provide protection to the worker against all the vicissitudes of industrial life—though at first sight socially desirable—brings in its train more disadvantages than advantages. Sophists argue that industrial justice would necessitate the imposition of innumerable regulations and prohibitions on industry which might stifle initiative and (extravagantly) reduce the rate of economic growth. Hence the responsibility for coping with such rough-edged economic phenomena as periodic unemployment, short-time working and the loss of income due to sickness, should lie with the worker himself. Once having secured a job he ought then, thriftily, to save sufficient money to cushion himself against hazard.

This extreme individualistic point of view now has fewer vocal exponents. Yet the view that the State ought not to intervene very much in the employment relationship is strongly held by many who speak and write on the subject of British industrial relations. They believe that if economic freedom is to be maintained each employer must be free within wide limits to conduct his business as he thinks best. The weight of argument is for the employer to retain untrammelled freedom of decision over a wide range of labour matters which affect the operation of his undertaking. Many employers in particular feel reluctant to accept obligations which in their view would prejudice what they choose to describe as their managerial rights. For this reason they seek to retain for themselves the maximum amount of freedom in relation to the termination of the employment of their employees.

This does not, of course, have much to do with the "round table" approach. It has everything to do with class tensions. Workers see it from this point of view. They are principally interested in security of employment and the continuity of their earnings. Wage and salary earners attach great importance to job security.

The relationship between an employer and an employee is not one between equals. The employer is in a much more powerful economic position than the employee. In many countries it has been recognised that, in order to redress to some extent this imbalance between employer and employee, the State in addition to protecting the workers' right of trade union organisation, also has a responsibility to protect the worker against some of the hardships of dismissal—and to give him some of the security which he needs. Today, many countries have legislation to regulate dismissal and lay-off procedures. Until the Contracts of Employment Act was placed on the statute book Britain was, again typically, one of the few countries where no legislation on the subject existed.

A recent ILO report—*Termination of Employment* (*Dismissal and Lay-off*), Report VII (1) Geneva 1961—said that the countries where legislation is the main source of regulation—although it is sometimes supplemented by collective agreements—include Afghanistan, Albania, Argentina, Austria, Belgium, Bolivia, Brazil, Bulgaria, Cameroun, Central African Republic, Ceylon, Chad, Chile, Colombia, Congo, Costa Rica, Cuba, Czechoslovakia, Dahomey, Dominican Republic, Ecuador, Finland, France, Gabon, Federal Republic of Germany, Greece, Guatemala, Guinea, Haiti, Honduras, Hungary, India, Iran, Iraq, Italy, Ivory Coast, Japan, Jordan, Lebanon, Libya, Malagasy Republic, Federation of Malaya, Mali, Mexico, Morocco, Netherlands, Nicaragua, Nigeria, Norway, Pakistan, Panama, Paraguay, Peru, Philippines, Poland, Portugal, Rumania, El Salvador, Senegal, Somalia, Spain, Sudan, Switzerland, Thailand, Togo, Tunisia, Turkey, USSR, United Arab Republic, Upper Volta, Uruguay, Venezuela, Viet-Nam, and Yugoslavia. In a number of other countries legislation determines dismissal procedures for salaried employees but not for manual workers. In Australia and New Zealand, arbitration awards are the main source of regulation for the termination of employment.

Change in the Climate of Opinion

The extent to which there has been a change in opinion in Britain towards the regulation of dismissal procedure was shown by the publication in 1961 of a Ministry of Labour booklet entitled *Security and Change*. Its foreword was written by the then Conservative Minister of Labour, Mr. John Hare. He said that the essence of the problem was how to reconcile the worker's natural desire for security in his job with the variations in the demand for labour caused by trading conditions and technical change. The worker, he pointed out, could not be expected to develop a sense of corporate loyalty to the firm for which he worked without some assurance that the firm accepted responsibility towards him in changing as well as in stable times.

Even in conditions of full employment or near full employment it is not possible to keep every worker in the same job throughout his working life. Changes are inevitable. Some industries will expand whilst others contract. Even in industries where the total labour force remains much the same there will be some occupations that will grow whilst others will decline. Thus whatever the state of employment hundreds of thousands of workers will find it necessary to change their jobs every year. It should be a pillar of State policy that society has an obligation to minimise the hardship caused as a result of these changes. The cost of compensation for loss of employment, resettlement allowances and retraining schemes should be regarded as a legitimate charge against the benefits of economic progress.

Some of the redundancies which occur in industry will be the result of increasing mechanisation and automation. This will affect not only the firms where these improvements in production methods are introduced but also the firms which fail to modernise. The sales of their products are likely to decline because of the more effective competition from the highly mechanised firms. It is often overlooked that technological unemployment is likely to arise at least as much in the firms which fail to modernise as in those that do. The fact that it is indirect rather than direct does not mean that there is any real difference in the cause of the unemployment. Workers are being displaced because of industrial changes—often spurred by national economic policy.

There will also be some industries where employment declines because of a change in demand or because of increased imports from abroad. Certain kinds of finished textiles, for example, are being manufactured increasingly from man-made fibres. At one time Britain was the world's principal exporter of textile goods. Now she imports substantial quantities from India, Pakistan, Hong Kong, Italy and other countries.

Changes in government policy may also materially affect employment in an industry. Thus, for example, the attitude of the government of the day towards the building of military aircraft and missiles and towards the construction of supersonic civil aircraft is bound to influence the level of employment in the aircraft industry.

The Ministry of Labour report on manpower entitled *The Pattern of the Future,* published in 1964, showed how the distribution of labour changes between one industry or service and another over a period of a decade. In the 10 years between 1953 and 1963 employment in the group of industries described as metal manufacture, engineering and shipbuilding rose by over 400,000, employment in textiles dropped over the same 10 years by over 200,000 and employment in the distributive trades rose by nearly 700,000. Changes have continued since that time. Some of these changes in the labour force would, of course, be accommodated by retirements and by the recruitment of new entrants from school. Even so, during every year hundreds of thousands of workers find it necessary to change not only their jobs but also their industry and occupations.

How to Alleviate Hardship

The hardships caused by industrial changes leading to redundancy can take many forms. The most obvious is the loss of earnings during the period immediately following the loss of employment. Hardship may, however, also be suffered by workers who find new employment almost immediately. They may find it necessary to take a job at a lower rate of pay or a long way from home, resulting in increased travelling expenses. If they have to travel to another town they may be put to the expense of finding lodgings or they may even find it necessary to buy or rent new accommodation. This may, in turn, lead to expense for new furniture, curtains and other fittings.

Agent's fees for buying and selling property may also have to be paid. A worker who changes his job can find that his pension provisions have been worsened, even though his earnings are much the same as before.

Apart from the direct financial loss that might be suffered as a result of redundancy there are other hardships with which the worker and his family are confronted. If it is necessary for the family to change its place of residence there may be a partial break-up of family life. There may also be a special problem if children are at school. A disturbance in the education of children can be extremely upsetting. There are many workers who, when faced with redundancy, have preferred to take a job near their home with lower earnings rather than move elsewhere for a job with higher earnings. To have moved elsewhere would have necessitated their children having to change schools.

All this indicates that the distress caused by redundancy and a change of employment can be very considerable and cannot be measured merely by calculating the loss of earnings in the period of unemployment immediately following redundancy. It lends weight to the argument that specific protection ought to be given to the worker who is faced with threatened redundancy.

Progress has been made in recent years in public measures to help meet the problems and effects of redundancy. The measures have been designed to cushion the effect of redundancy on the workers concerned and to facilitate the transfer of workers to other suitable employment.

Redundancy Payments Act

In addition to the Contracts of Employment Act, 1963, which gives workers a legal entitlement to longer periods of notice based on length of service, there is now the Redundancy Payments Act, 1965. This provides for lump sum payments to be made to redundant workers with at least 2 years' service with their employer. The scale of payments is as follows:

For each year of employment between ages 18 and 21	$\frac{1}{2}$ week's pay
For each year of employment between ages 22 and 40	1 week's pay
For each year of employment between ages 41 and 64	$1\frac{1}{2}$ week's pay

For purposes of calculating the redundancy payment, service is limited to the last 20 years before redundancy. Earnings above £40 a week are disregarded. Thus the maximum sum that can be paid is £1200. This would be paid to a worker with 20 years' service with an employer all beyond the age of 40, and with earnings of £40 per week. For the purpose of the Act an employee is dismissed because of redundancy where the whole or main reason for his dismissal is that his employer's needs for employees to do work of a particular kind have diminished or ceased. If the employer claims that the reason for dismissal is other than redundancy the onus of proof rests on him and not on the worker.

The Redundancy Payments Act established a Redundancy Fund financed by contributions collected with the employer's National Insurance contributions. When making a redundancy payment to a redundant employee an employer is entitled to claim a rebate of part of the cost from the Fund. From 1 January 1966 to 31 December 1966, redundancy payments made under the Act amounted to £26,488,000, of which £19,876,000 was borne by the Fund and £6,612,000 paid directly by employers. The number of payments made during the year was 137,208.

Earnings-related Benefit

Another measure which has helped to cushion many workers against some of the worst effects of redundancy is the earnings-related supplement to unemployment benefit. This was introduced in late 1966 under the National Insurance Act, 1966. The supplements are payable to unemployed persons who are entitled to flat-rate unemployment benefit and who have earnings of at least £450 in the relevant tax year.

The supplement is payable at the rate of one-third of the amount of average weekly earnings which exceed £9 a week and are less than £30 a week. The supplement is payable for up to 6 months of unemployment in addition to flat-rate benefit including increases for dependants. There is a maximum total benefit of 85 per cent of average earnings.

Though the new earnings-related benefit scheme has helped many workers it has done nothing for the lower paid. The position of the unemployed workers who were lowly paid in their last job is an extremely difficult one. It is, of course, linked with the whole question of the need for improved provision for lower paid workers, particularly those with large families.

Training and Retraining

When workers are made redundant the best solution is for other work to be available for them. If the available work is near to their home, if it utilises the skills which the workers possess and if it offers a rate of pay not less than that paid in their last job the disturbance caused by the change of employment will be reduced to a minimum. The real problems arise when there is no such combination of favourable circumstances. It is then that redundant workers must be retrained for new skills and must be assisted to transfer their homes to other areas where jobs are available.

The tradition in Britain is for industry itself to conduct its own training of workers. There are relatively few training schools maintained by private firms. The great majority of workers are trained on production processes. The standards of training vary enormously from firm to firm. The best firms provide good training arrangements but in far too many the training is haphazard.

In 1964 Parliament passed the Industrial Training Act with a view to bringing about a much needed improvement in the standards of training throughout British industry. The Act empowers the Minister of Labour to set up industrial training boards. The purpose of these boards is to secure better training in industry, to ensure an adequate supply of properly trained men and women at all levels in industry and to make arrangements for sharing the cost of training more evenly between firms. Boards covering more than 10 million workers are now in existence. A number of these boards are encouraging adult re-training schemes. The rates of levy imposed by the different boards show considerable differences one with the other. So too do the grants. This reflects the different needs of different sections of industry.

This effort to improve standards of training is needed and is welcome, but there should be no complacency about its effectiveness. The whole scheme depends, in the ultimate, on the voluntary co-operation of firms even though through a system of levies and grants the boards can encourage training and discourage firms who are content to leave it to others. Within a few years all industry and trade will be covered by training boards. Industrial training will need to be integrated with the education system with part-time day release for all young workers under 18 years of age.

The Government also provide training facilities in their own training centres. More than thirty are in existence and it is hoped to have thirty-eight by the end of 1967. These facilities are being expanded to turn out nearly 15,000 trained people a year. The centres provide training opportunities for men who missed the chance to learn a skill or, perhaps because of redundancy, find it necessary to learn a new skill. More than forty different trades are taught. Courses last, on average, for about 6 months though the training is longer for the more skilled trades. The training is intensive and is very well organised. Trainees receive maintenance grants during training and, if eligible for earnings-related supplementary unemployment benefit, draw a supplementary grant Unions have been co-operative, with few exceptions, in accepting trainees into employment.

Firms setting up or expanding in Development Areas are also eligible for training grants from the Government. If a firm trains workers on its own premises it can claim a grant of £5 a week for each male trainee over 18 and £2 10s. 0d. a week for each male trainee under 18. The grant for women trainees over 18 is £3 10s. 0d. and for girls under 18 is £2. Ministry of Labour staff is also provided free of charge to assist in the starting of training schemes.

The Ministry of Labour take special steps through the employment exchange service to help redundant workers to find new jobs. When redundancy is imminent firms are asked to notify the Ministry of Labour so that inquiries can be made about other available work so that the list of vacant jobs is as comprehensive as possible. The Ministry also have experienced placing officers who are made available when substantial numbers of workers have been made redundant.

Early in 1966 the Ministry of Labour also established an occupational guidance scheme for adults. The scheme provides a service for adults who face an enforced change of occupation because, say, of redundancy, who feel that they are under-employed and voluntarily seek a new job, who are unsettled in their work or who are entering employment for the first time or returning to it—for example married women –after an absence of some years. In July 1967 the Minister of Labour announced that there was to be an expansion of the occupational guidance scheme.

Unemployed workers who cannot get jobs within daily travelling distance from their homes are eligible for financial help from the State to take a job in another area. This assistance can also be given to workers who will be made redundant within a period of 6 months. The assistance may be on a very limited scale and may amount to the fare to the new area plus £5 settling-in allowance. Information about these schemes is available at Ministry of Labour employment exchanges. On the other hand, a man with dependants may receive a lodging allowance of £3 10s. 0d. a week and assistance for fares for visits to his home. Assistance can also be provided towards removal costs, legal costs for the sale and purchase of a house, dependants' fares and other small expenses.

These measures of assistance provided by the State have done something to mitigate the blow of redundancy. It is *easy*, however, for persons who have never had to face redundancy to slip into the assumption that ambulance work of this kind is all that is necessary. To the majority of workers it is still a severe blow to be made redundant.

Regulation of Dismissal

Apart from the Acts on contracts of employment and redundancy pay such safeguards as exist in Britain for the *regulation* of dismissal are provided in collective agreements. Such provisions in private industry are few and severely limited in scope. The plain fact is that the great majority of workers are not covered by agreements on dismissal procedure or redundancy despite the fact that it has now been the policy of successive governments for a number of years to encourage such agreements.

The Ministry of Labour booklet *Security and Change* said in 1961 that plans for dealing with possible redundancy in the future should be regarded as part of the normal responsibility of management. Nevertheless, according to a survey conducted by the Ministry of Labour, the results of which were published in the *Ministry of Labour Gazette* for February 1963, only about $4\frac{1}{2}$ million workers were covered by redundancy provisions. A large majority of this number were in public employment, including the nationalised industries. In private manufacturing industry five out of every six workers were employed by companies which had no redundancy policy. Even among the industries and firms which had made provision for redundancy, many of the arrangements were extremely limited in scope. Since the beginning of 1963 more firms have introduced or negotiated arrangements for redundancy. Even now, however, only a minority of the total labour force is covered by them.

It might be argued in reply to this criticism that one of the reasons why so few private industries have established arrangements for dealing with redundancy is that they have not been pressed to do so by the unions. There is some truth in this, though one of the principal reasons why some unions have not pressed for national redundancy agreements is that in their view when redundancy occurs in a firm more can often be obtained by local negotiations than by reference to a national agreement. A national agreement, they say, would be extremely modest and the benefits which it would confer on workers would be determined by what the most backward and least profitable firms in the industry would accept or could afford.

The Ministry of Labour's survey early in 1963 revealed that most of the workers who were covered by redundancy policies were employed in large firms. The Ministry pointed out that it was clearly the larger firms that, for the most part, felt it necessary or desirable to formulate a policy for dealing with redundancy. Unions can usually obtain better terms from large firms, where redundancy may affect only one department or establishment, than from agreements with employers' federations who have to take into account what is possible not only for the large firms but also for the small firms. Thus a national agreement with an employers' federation might, in practice, prejudice rather than help negotiations if and when redundancy occurs in a large firm.

Another argument which has been voiced in trade union circles to oppose the negotiation of national agreements on redundancy is that there is no such thing as a "good redundancy agreement". Every such agreement, it is said, is essentially a procedure for the sacking of workers. Hence the existence of a redundancy agreement takes the sting out of the struggle for the maintenance of employment.

This argument is not, in practice, so futile as it may seem. There are a number of examples where threatened redundancy has not materialised because the energetic campaigning of the workers directly affected has led to other temporary solutions being adopted. New orders have eventually been received and employment has been maintained.

These trade union arguments against national agreements, though they certainly cannot be dismissed lightly as some outside commentators have attempted in the past, derive their strength from present circumstances. They relate essentially to the relative advantage of local activity and negotiations as against national agreements. They are not an argument against the placing of statutory obligations on all employers.

The proportion of workers covered by redundancy arrangements varies very much from one private industry to another. In chemicals and in vehicle manufacture the proportion covered by redundancy arrangements was, according to the Ministry of Labour survey in 1963, respectively 48 per cent and 32 per cent of the total workforce. In a wide range of manufacturing industries the proportion covered by redundancy arrangements was very much smaller.

Another interesting feature revealed by the Ministry survey was that less than a half of the redundancy policies in existence were adopted after consultation with employees' representatives and only a very few were embodied in formal signed agreements. All the other arrangements were adopted by managements acting by themselves.

Arbitrary Dismissal

In the agreements on redundancy arrangements, redundancy is generally defined as the involuntary loss of a job through no fault of the worker concerned. There is missing in Britain, from legislation or in collective agreements, the idea that the worker should be entitled *as a social right* to keep his job unless there are special reasons to justify his dismissal. In other words, the concept here even among progressively minded people, has been generally to provide for the alleviation of the situation of a worker who faces redundancy but not to restrict the employer's freedom of dismissal *as such*. There has been little canvassing of the proposition that dismissal should not take place unless there are adequate and acceptable reasons for it.

It is still the case that a British worker can be dismissed subject only to proper notice, but without legal redress, at the mere whim of the employer and without any stated reason. In many industries such a dismissal would be resisted vigorously by the trade union covering the worker concerned. Redress would be sought through the process of collective bargaining. There is, however, no *legal* provision which gives safeguards to workers against arbitrary dismissal.

In its 1964 General Election manifesto the Labour Party promised, in its proposed charter of rights, to introduce safeguards against arbitrary dismissal for all employees. Such safeguards already exist in the legislation of many other countries. The underlying principle there is that a dismissed worker should have the right to challenge his dismissal on the grounds that it is "unjustified". This challenge is usually offered in the first place through the normal machinery of collective bargaining, but if no satisfactory settlement is reached it can be pursued through a labour court, arbitration body or other institution endowed with the right to examine and make an award.

Arbitrary Dismissal—the Law in Other Countries

The April 1963 issue of the *Ministry of Labour Gazette* contained a survey of redundancy arrangements in a number of west European countries and in the USA. This account, which supplemented information on the subject given in the ILO report *Termination of Employment*, confirmed that in western Europe it is customary to provide legislative safeguards against "abusive" dismissal.

In France, for example, any employer who wishes to dismiss an employee for any reason is required to request permission to do so from the manpower service in his area. An exception is made in the case of the liberal professions, agriculture, and industries such as civil engineering and building where there is a rapid turnover of labour. There is, however, strict control in manufacturing industry. In general the employers have the right to dismiss individual employees, but there must not be "abuse" of this right or an employer may be liable for damages. The Ministry of Labour in France may also refuse permission for workers to be discharged.

In Belgium the concept of "abusive dismissal" is also incorporated in the law. In Germany, workers are protected against what is described as "socially unwarranted dismissal". This is defined in German law as "any dismissal not based on reasons connected with the person, or the conduct of the employee, or pressing operational requirements which preclude his continued employment in the undertaking".

The law in the Netherlands also protects workers against arbitrary dismissal. A worker may be awarded damages or, under certain circumstances, reinstatement if he is dismissed in a manner which is manifestly unreasonable. A dismissal may be regarded as manifestly unreasonable if the consequences to the worker outweigh the advantages of such dismissal to the employer, or if the worker is dismissed in contravention of a legislative provision or custom relating to staff composition or seniority rules.

In Italy, the protection of workers against unjustified dismissal rested until July 1966 on a national collective agreement. It applied to undertakings with more than thirty-five workers. A worker who considered that he had been unjustifiably dismissed could request the intervention of his trade union and could take the case to a conciliation and arbitration procedure. In July 1966 a new law was promulgated establishing the principle that a worker may not be dismissed without valid reason. It was described in the March 1967 issue of the *International Labour Review*:

> On 15th July 1966 an Act was promulgated in Italy establishing new principles concerning dismissal, and introducing the principle that a worker may not be dismissed without valid reason. The new Act deals only with dismissal with notice, summary dismissal being dealt with in the Civil Code (article 2119). The main provisions of the new Act are as follows:

"Every dismissal must be communicated to the worker concerned by the employer in writing. Within eight days of this communication the worker may request that the employer give him, within five days, the reasons on which the dismissal is based.

"Valid reasons for dismissal are a notable failure of the employee to comply with his contractual obligations, or reasons relating to the production process, the organisation of the work and its regular functioning. Any dismissal based on grounds of political or religious opinion, trade union membership and participation in trade union activities is null and void. The employer must show evidence of the existence of a valid reason for dismissal.

"Within 60 days of receiving notice, the worker may object to the dismissal. The means of recourse include procedures provided by collective agreements, conciliation by the labour authorities, arbitration and court decisions.

"If it is found that the notice indicated for the dismissal does not constitute a valid reason the employer must reinstate the worker within three days or, failing this, pay him an indemnity of at least five and at most 12 months' salary, taking into account the size of the undertaking, the length of service of the worker and the attitude of the parties. The maximum amount of the indemnity is reduced to eight months' wages for workers with less than 30 months' seniority and may be increased to 14 months' wages for workers with more than 20 years' service. For employers with up to 60 employees the minimum and maximum amounts of the indemnity are reduced to one-half.

"The law specifies that the seniority indemnity is payable to workers in all cases of termination of employment.

"It does not apply to employers with up to 35 employees or to workers who have become entitled to an old-age pension or those who are more than 65 years old; these exceptions do not apply as regards the prohibition of dismissal for reasons of political or religious opinion, trade union membership and participation in trade union activities."

The ILO report entitled *Termination of Employment* refers also to the example of Norway. It says that under Norwegian legislation an employer who dismisses a worker without a well-founded reason must pay compensation or must reinstate him. This applies only to workers who have been employed for at least 2 years without interruption in the same establishment after attaining the age of 20 years. According to Norwegian law a well-founded reason for dismissal is one which is inherent in the circumstance of the owner of the establishment, the worker, or the establishment itself. Many decisions have since been made by the courts to give a closer definition of what constitutes a well-founded reason. The ILO report says that, in general, a dismissal can be regarded as well-founded if it takes place after careful consideration of the operational needs of the undertaking. Reasons accepted as well-founded by court decisions include rationalisation, reduction in output, violation of discipline, negligence, old age, frequent absenteeism and, in certain cases, sickness.

A study of the problem of justification of dismissal by E. Hertz, published in the *International Labour Review* in April 1954, stated:

> ... in an increasing number of countries the will of the employer standing by itself is no longer regarded as an adequate reason for ending the employment relationship. It is being accepted more and more that an employer wishing to dissolve the contract of employment must state the grounds of his action and that the worker may have the validity of these investigated by an authority independent of both parties.

Proposal for a New Law

A safeguard against arbitrary dismissal in Britain could be provided by legislation which gave workers the right to appeal against any proposed sacking. The appeal could be made in the first place by the worker's trade union through the normal process of collective bargaining. If it were unsuccessful and if the union wished to pursue the appeal before independent persons, as opposed to taking industrial action, it could then go to an industrial court. When an appeal was instituted an obligation ought to be placed on the employer to prove the justification for the dismissal. As the ILO report *Termination of Employment* points out, it is of great practical importance whether the worker must prove that his dismissal was unjustified or whether the employer must prove its justification. In the Federal Republic of Germany, for instance, the law insists that the employer must prove the facts on which the dismissal is based. This principle ought to be embodied in British legislation. A step in the right direction was taken by the Redundancy Payments Act, 1965—referred to earlier—which places the onus of proof on an employer should he claim that a worker has been dismissed for reasons other than redundancy.

The experience of other countries suggests that as far as the labour courts are concerned the grounds for justifiable dismissal fall into three broad categories. First, there are those connected with the lack of skill of the worker; for example, his incapacity or his incompetence. Secondly, there are those connected with the conduct of the worker, as for example, indiscipline or persistent lateness or absenteeism. Thirdly there are those connected with the operation of the undertaking, as for example rationalisation, mechanisation, or a fall in demand.

Whilst any or all of these reasons may be regarded by a labour court as providing sufficient grounds for dismissal a trade union may, nevertheless, contest them on grounds of broad social policy. A union might not accept, for example, that redundancy is inevitable because of mechanisation or automation. It might instead urge that hours of work should be cut. Nothing in the proposed new legislation ought to prevent a union from resisting redundancy by normal trade union means if it so chooses. In other words, the normal process of collective bargaining and trade union pressure would not in all cases be followed by the procedure of appeal before an industrial court. It would be for the union to decide whether an appeal should be submitted to an industrial court if the negotiations with the employer and employers' federation had been exhausted and had been abortive. Alternatively, the union might decide on some form of industrial action—and it should be free to do so—to press its point of view.

In a case, for example, concerning the alleged victimisation of a worker for trade union activity a union may prefer to call an immediate strike rather than to await the submission of an appeal to an industrial court. Victimisation is always difficult to prove and usually the only effective answer to it is for the colleagues of the victimised worker to withdraw their labour to show that they want him to continue as their representative.

The importance of providing a legal check on dismissal is not only that it affords a means of redress for workers who are unjustifiably dismissed but its very existence also serves as a restraining influence on employers. At present in Britain an employer who is contemplating dismissing workers knows that it is a matter entirely for his own decision, unless those who work for him are members of a trade union and are actively represented by the union. The potential use of force is the only sanction in favour of justice. There are many employers who dismiss workers without taking into account anything other than their own commercial convenience. If, however, there were legislation to provide a safeguard against arbitrary dismissal employers would be much more likely to hesitate and to consider all the relevant circumstances before issuing discharge notices. They might well have to plan much better.

Comprehensive Legislation

Much still remains to be done to provide proper protection for the worker who is dismissed or who is threatened with dismissal. The Contracts of Employment Act provides the barest minimum of protection for workers with more than two years' service with an employer. The Redundancy Payments Act was an important step forward towards the mitigation of the effects of redundancy, but it has a number of defects and its scale of lump sum payments is not generous. In Italy, for example, where provision for indemnity payments to workers whose services are terminated, except for dismissal on the grounds of misconduct, has existed since 1942, it is the general practice for collective agreements to grant an allowance equal to one month's wage or salary for every year of service.

The Redundancy Payments Act also permits employers in certain circumstances to set off pensions or lump sums which are paid on redundancy against the redundancy payment to which the worker is entitled by law. According to the amount of the pension or lump sum paid from a superannuation fund the redundancy payment due may be either reduced or extinguished completely. Employers, it should be noted, are not compelled to act in this way but, needless to say, many of them do. It seems thoroughly unfair. Undoubtedly part of the problem is created by the lack of employees' rights in many private occupational pension schemes. If employers were compelled to pay the full redundancy payment the argument is that some of them would not exercise their powers in relation to occupational pensions to the advantage of employees. The answer is surely to tighten up the law in relation to private occupational pension schemes so that the rights of employees are properly protected.

The earnings-related unemployment benefit scheme has also helped the better paid redundant worker. The lowly paid redundant worker, particularly if he has children, continues to exist in poverty. A substantial increase in family allowances, together with much higher minimum rates in employment would help towards eliminating this social problem. There ought also to be an adequate subsistence level of National Insurance benefits. Unemployed workers who claim supplementary allowances are still subject to the "wages stop". This discretionary power enables the State to withhold part of the allowance of a worker because his usual earnings are lower than his assessed requirements. The redundant workers who suffer under this provision are precisely those who already live in poverty even when in employment.

The new unemployment benefit scheme also retains the three waiting days for flat rate benefit and introduced a twelve day waiting period for the earnings related supplement. The General Council of the TUC urged—in our view rightly so—that the waiting period for flat rate benefit should be abolished and that the waiting period for supplementary benefit was too long.

Legislation on the dismissal of the worker ought not to be limited to minimum periods of notice, redundancy payments, provision for training and retraining and unemployment benefit. In addition, legislation is needed to provide redress against unjustifiable dismissal.

Legislation is also needed to place upon employers an obligation to consult workpeople's representatives whenever dismissals are contemplated. This should apply to all types of dismissal, including dismissals for indiscipline or dismissals—more commonly known as redundancy—caused by changes in economic circumstances.

This obligation to consult would do much to encourage employers to work for the three basic objectives on redundancy arrangements described in the Ministry of Labour booklet *Security and Change*. These tasks were:

> to prevent redundancy by the forward planning of labour requirements;
> to make advance plans for dealing with possible redundancy and to ensure that the workers concerned know what these are;
> to make special provision to reduce the hardships caused to individuals.

The placing of an obligation on employers to consult workers' representative on dismissals would encourage works committees and works councils of every kind to consider the forward planning of labour requirements. An employer can do a great deal to adjust the size of his labour force to anticipated requirements without the necessity of dismissals. Planning will be all the more effective—and acceptable—if it takes into account the views expressed by the workers' representatives.

As the Ministry of Labour booklet stated, "The employer can consider his policies of recruitment, training, promotion and retirement in the light of long term labour requirements at all levels. With the help of such planning, recruitment can be regulated against normal wastage."

If it appears likely that there will be a slackening of demand for a particular product, a firm may be able to transfer workers from one department to another. It may also avoid redundancy by eliminating overtime or even by introducing short-time working for a brief period. A firm may also help to maintain full employment for its existing workers by withdrawing work from sub-contractors.

The forward planning of labour requirements not only corresponds to the need of workers for security but also makes good sense to the employers. The Engineering Employers' Federation, in a memorandum on policies and procedure for dealing with redundancy issued in May 1963, stated: "The Federation considers that in an age where both demand and methods of production change very rapidly all federated firms should have some precise ideas as to how redundancy should be handled should it arise."

The obligation on employers to consult workers' representatives on all dismissals ought to be coupled with an obligation to inform the Ministry of Labour. Steps could then be taken by the Ministry, either on their own initiative or in co-operation with the employer and union representatives, to do whatever might be possible to help in finding new jobs for redundant workers whilst they were *still* in employment and *before* their dismissal.

If legislation were introduced in Britain to provide safeguards against arbitrary dismissal, to place an obligation upon employers to consult workers' representatives, to notify the Ministry of Labour when dismissals were contemplated, and to provide more generous severance payments to workers who were dismissed through no fault of their own, a framework would be created for reducing the hardships that follow from redundancy in industry.

Redundancy and Collective Bargaining

Legislation on redundancy on the lines outlined above would still leave much to be discussed within the machinery of collective bargaining. There would, for example, be a need for employers and unions to negotiate arrangements to help workers facing redundancy to seek new employment. Time off during the warning period and during the period of notice should be given for this purpose. Negotiations would also be necessary to provide for the longest possible period of warning of impending redundancy. The survey of white collar redundancy, which was conducted by Mrs. Dorothy Wedderburn at the English Electric factory at Stevenage* showed that adequate advance warning of redundancy is very important. Workers who find new jobs as a result of this advance warning ought not to lose their entitlement to redundancy payments. Employers and unions would also have to consider

* *White-collar Redundancy—A Case Study* by Dorothy Wedderburn, Cambridge University Press.

T.K.L.U.O.W—D

writing into redundancy agreements provisions for priority of re-engagement for workers who are dismissed.

In their memorandum on recommended policies and procedure for dealing with redundancy issued in 1963 the Engineering Employers' Federation suggested that when redundancy is clearly inevitable a three-stage programme to give effect to the discharges should be adopted. The first stage, it was suggested, should comprise the period from the time when a general warning of impending redundancy is given up to the time when the workpeople selected for discharge are first individually warned to that effect. The second stage should comprise the period during which the workers concerned are under individual warning that notice of termination of employment is to be given. The third stage should consist of the actual period of notice itself. Thus the advice given by the Engineering Employers' Federation to their member firms confirms the need for as long a warning period as possible to be given to workers who might be affected.

The principles to be observed in selecting workers for dismissals also provide plenty of scope for negotiations. In some instances it has been the practice to operate the principle of "last in—first out". Sometimes the unions have felt that this provides a safeguard against the victimisation of active trade unionists. Furthermore, it is a principle which can be readily understood by all workers. When redundancy is threatened justice has not only to be done but, in the words of the well-known saying, it has also to be seen to be done. Workers should be able to understand clearly the grounds on which some of their number are being selected for discharge. Employers, on the other hand, sometimes take the view that the principle of "last in—first out" obliges them to dismiss workers who are efficient or who are good timekeepers. "Last in—first out" may also require them to retain workers who are less competent or who have a record of lateness or persistent absenteeism.

There is no principle which can be applied equally to all circumstances. Every case of redundancy has to be considered on its merits. The principle of "last in—first out" is usually a useful starting point for negotiations. It can then be modified in the light of local circumstances. Workers readily recognise that colleagues who have special family responsibilities or who have physical disabilities may have a claim for retention of employment. Workers' representatives should also have protection because of their exposed position.

There is, too, the whole problem of the retraining of redundant workers. In some large firms it is also possible for the employers and unions to negotiate arrangements under which workers made redundant in one department or one occupation may be given the opportunity to train for new employment in another department or in another occupation.

Legislation and Collective Bargaining

So far Britain has been backward in dealing with the problems of redundancy. These problems need to be dealt with and, as far as possible, overcome by a combination of legislative and collective bargaining provisions. Neither one nor the other alone is sufficient. The introduction of legislation on the lines described in previous paragraphs would help to reduce the hardships of redundancy and would also encourage the further development of collective bargaining arrangements for the planning of manpower requirements and for the protection of the worker.

There is no court or tribunal in the United Kingdom with the power to order the reinstatement of a worker. All that it can do is to ensure that the worker is given proper notice.*

This will not do. The power should now be created to order the reinstatement of a worker who has been unjustifiably dismissed. This power should be vested in a body such as the existing Industrial Tribunals. Criteria should also be established as to what constitutes a "socially unjustified" dismissal.

---

* As this book was going to press the Ministry of Labour published a report on dismissal procedures from a committee of the National Joint Advisory Council. It is an informative report but argues, on balance, against legislation. The TUC, we are glad to note, considered that there should be legislation on the subject.

CHAPTER 6

The portable pension problem

THE idea that elderly people who have retired from labour have a claim, as of right, upon the current income of society is of comparatively recent origin. In earlier centuries it was considered that elderly people should continue at work or should depend upon help from their relatives if they had not saved sufficient from their life's labour to maintain themselves in old age. If these means of support were not possible or were not available old people could apply, as a last resort, for Poor Law relief. Today's social atmosphere is better but it leaves a great deal to be desired and accomplished both for blue-collar and non-manual workers.

A Brief History

The system of Poor Law relief originated with the Poor Relief Act of 1601. Each parish was made responsible for the maintenance of its poor: work was to be provided for those capable of labour. Those who were incapable, because of infirmity, age or mental weakness, were to be maintained. The severity of the system varied from one period to another but the general principle observed was that each man should maintain himself and his immediate family by his own efforts. If he failed to do so because of laziness he was to be punished. If he failed to do so for other reasons, including old age, he could expect some support from the community, but this support was given in such a way that it offered no attraction to anyone and served as an example to all to provide for themselves. For many decades old people who were destitute had to depend on "outdoor-relief" which barely kept them alive, or they had to submit to the rigours of the workhouse.

The first substantial break with the Poor Law system came with Lloyd George's Old Age Pensions Act, 1908. This provided for non-contributory pensions of 5*s.* per week for people over 70 years of age. It was paid subject to a test of means. In 1920 the non-contributory pension was increased to 10*s.* a week.

In 1925 the Widows', Orphans' and Old Age Contributory Pensions Act was passed. This introduced the contributory principle. The 1925 Act provided for the payment of a pension of 10*s.* per week to contributors, both men and women, from the age of 65. The payment of a pension from the age of 70 remained non-contributory. The 1925 Act was subsequently extended in 1937 to provide voluntary insurance to many white-collar workers who previously had not been within the scope of the contributory scheme.

In 1940 the age at which a woman could qualify for a contributory pension was reduced to 60 years. This was done, it was said, so that wives, who were on average about 4 years younger than their husbands, could qualify for pensions at the same time as their partners, and also as a concession to unmarried women. In 1940 provision was also made for the Assistance Board, which was a statutory national body previously concerned with unemployment assistance, to pay supplementary pensions, subject to a test of means, to both contributory and non-contributory pensioners. Until 1940 Poor Law relief remained the only source of support for old people who were unable to live on their pensions and who had no other resources.

The whole system of social security was recast after the Second World War on the broad lines recommended in the 1942 Beveridge Report. A comprehensive contributory insurance scheme was introduced to include retirement pensions. The old Poor Law system finally came to an end in 1948 with the passing of the National Assistance Act. This created a national system of cash allowances administered by the National Assistance Board. The allowances were to be available to everyone in need. Outdoor relief and supplementary pensions were replaced by National Assistance cash allowances.

The 1946 National Insurance Act was based on four fundamental principles.

> *First:* that the system of social security should be comprehensive. It should be the social right of every citizen to enjoy security, and the benefits should not be subject to a means test.
>
> *Second:* that the benefits should be sufficient to maintain a family at an acceptable subsistence level without assistance from any other source.
>
> *Third:* that the scheme should be financed partly by the State from taxation and partly by contributions from employers and employees.
>
> *Fourth:* that the contributions and benefits should be flat-rate, i.e. the same amount from and for everyone.

The Present Position

Since the National Insurance scheme was first introduced the important principle that the benefits should be sufficient to maintain a family without assistance from any other source has gradually been undermined. Some improvement was, however, made as a result of the increases in National Insurance benefit introduced by the Labour Government in October 1964 and the changes made by the Social Security Act 1966 and the National Insurance Act 1966. Nevertheless, in order to maintain a minimum level of subsistence millions of people each year had to apply for National Assistance cash allowances to supplement National Insurance benefits. The National Assistance Board was conceived as the safety net under the national social security system: it became the bedrock of it.

The Social Security Act of 1966 provided for a new scheme of non-contributory benefits to replace National Assistance. This was of special importance to pensioners, the unemployed, the sick and disabled, widows, deserted wives and unmarried mothers. The main purpose of the new scheme was to give a form of guaranteed income to elderly people and others who require benefit over a long period. Persons of pensionable age receive a "supplementary pension" and others a "supplementary allowance". These benefits are established as a right to be claimed by everyone entitled to them. Persons ineligible for national insurance retirement pension are eligible equally with retirement pensioners to claim the supplementary pension.

Under the new scheme a person receiving a supplementary pension and living alone as a householder is entitled to a guaranteed income, after paying his nett rent and rates, of £4. 10s. 0d. a week. A married couple living alone, after they have paid their nett rent and rates, are entitled to a guaranteed income of £7. 2s. 0d. a week. Provision is made under the scheme for disregarding certain small items of income and capital when calculating the amount of benefit to which a claimant is entitled. The new Supplementary Benefits Commission also have discretionary power to increase a supplementary pension to meet special needs.

By changes in the financing of the National Insurance scheme and the National Health Service a disproportionate share of the burden has been placed on families with low incomes. A pamphlet produced by the TUC in 1961, *Who is Paying for Social Security ?*, pointed out that National Insurance contributions and Health Service charges had been substantially increased over the years. At the same time the Exchequer had been relieved of a large part of the cost of the National Health Service and of the emerging cost of the National Insurance scheme. The TUC pamphlet said:

> Step by step, over a period of years, the proportion of the rising costs of social security met out of public money raised by taxation has been shrinking. The proportion paid by the contributor and the patient, largely regardless of their income, has been increasing.

In his Fabian lecture, "Poverty, Socialism and Labour in Power", November 1966, Professor Peter Townsend pointed out that the increase in benefits in November 1964 was accompanied by steep increases in employees' contributions. This fell heavily on lowly paid workers:

> Moreover, the employees' flat rate contributions, which, according to the Labour Party only a year earlier, had already reached a level where they constitute a savage poll tax on the lowest paid workers, were increased by 17% from 11s. 8d. to 13s. 8d. a week.

Since the introduction of the post-war National Insurance scheme there has been a general change of opinion regarding the social desirability of flat rate contributions and benefits. The Labour Party's statement of policy entitled *New Frontiers for Social Security* outlined two main reasons for a radical break with the principle of flat-rate contributions and benefits contained in the original National Insurance scheme. The first reason was that wage-related contributions and benefits enable increases to be introduced without placing an enormous burden on the lowest paid workers. Flat-rate contributions, the Labour Party pointed out, had already reached a level where they constituted a savage tax on the lowest paid worker. Under a wage related benefit scheme a more highly paid worker might be prepared to pay a higher contribution if he knew that it would bring him a higher pension when he reached the age of 65.

The second reason for discarding the principle of flat rate contributions and benefits was that, to quote the Labour Party's statement, "The time has now come to rise above the concept of fair shares in poverty." Just as there are differences in income between working people when they are at work, so, the argument goes, there is no intrinsic reason why there should not be differences in income between them when they are retired, provided always, of course, that no-one is allowed to fall below a minimum level of subsistence.

The National Insurance Act of 1966 introduced into the National Insurance scheme a system of earnings-related supplements to unemployment and sickness benefit. An earnings-related supplementary allowance is now also payable in addition to the flat-rate widow's allowance. The cost of these supplements was met by new graduated contributions payable by employers and employees on the amount of earnings lying between £9 and £30 per week which were payable regardless of whether the employees were contracted out of the main graduated arrangements. They count for graduated pension in the same way as do the graduated contributions at present paid on earnings between £9 and £18—even where they are paid by those contracted out.

These arrangements took effect in the autumn of 1966 and were a welcome improvement in Britain's social security provisions. They helped to bridge the wide chasm between the workers' income while fully employed—particularly the better paid worker —and what he receives while out of work, on short time or retired.

The low level of National Insurance benefits, in the years immediately before this legislation, was underpinned by government encouragement to employers to develop their own private occupational pension schemes. The insurance companies benefited enormously from this expansion of business. The expansion was also stimulated by very generous tax concessions. It was estimated by the Government, according to a reply to a parliamentary question, that the cost to the Exchequer of tax relief on occupational pension schemes in 1962/3 was about £55 million on employees' contributions, £150 million on employers' contributions and £40 million on the investment income of superannuation funds.

In the second half of the 1950's the Labour Party formulated proposals for an ambitious scheme for State pensions in which both contributions and benefits would be related to the wage or salary level of the contributor. The proposals envisaged that private occupational pension schemes would be permitted to continue, provided that they offered terms as good as those of the proposed State scheme and provided they included arrangements for transferability when a worker changed his employment.

The Conservative Government then developed their own, though less ambitious, proposals. The essential point of the Conservative scheme was that it provided a supplementary graduated pension for contributors whose income was above a basic minimum. These contributors were required to pay additional graduated contributions. This graduated pension scheme was so framed that the benefits which it offered were less attractive than those provided in many occupational schemes run by insurance companies.

Under the graduated pension scheme it is possible for employees to be contracted out of the obligation to contribute for a supplementary graduated pension providing that they are members of an acceptable private pension scheme. To be acceptable for this purpose a private occupational pension scheme has to be financially sound, has to provide benefits at least equal to the best provided under the State scheme, and has to provide for employees changing their jobs for the preservation of pension rights equal to those which would have been secured had the contributor been in the State scheme. But there is no insistence that pension rights superior to those of the state scheme shall be preserved on change of employment. Herein is the hazard for so many persons wishing to leave a given employer.

Occupational Pension Schemes

It is estimated that about 13 million workers in British industry and commerce are now members of occupational pension schemes. Approximately 4 million of the total number of 13 million are employed in the public services of one kind or another, including the armed services, and in the nationalised industries. Probably rather more than one-half of all employed now have some provision for pensions other than those provided under National Insurance. The number in occupational pension schemes has been growing at the rate of half a million a year. This includes about two-thirds of all male workers between the ages of 20 and 65.

Surveys of occupational pension schemes, made by the Government Actuary in 1957/8, and again in 1963/4, showed how diverse and varied were the schemes then in existence. The report of the last survey said that the total number of active schemes in the private sector was believed to be in the range of 60,000. Many firms have more than one scheme for their different categories of employees.

The total cost of occupational pension provision is now running at a rate of more than £1000 million a year. The 1963/4 official survey suggested that members' and employers' contributions together, covering both the private and the public sector, amounted to about £850 million.

The total annual sum contributed by employers to these occupational pension schemes was more than twice as much as the amount contributed by employees. This, however, is not the normal ratio of payment as between employer and employee. The considerably higher level of employers' payments, probably arose, said the Government Actuary's survey, largely because of payments made by employers to extinguish deficiencies, notably those due to admitting existing staff of all ages on terms appropriate only to new recruits, and to granting a measure of "back service" rights.

Some private schemes, including the scheme in the civil service, do not require employees to make contributions. They are generally known as non-contributory schemes. In others, the employer makes a higher contribution than the employee. There are also many schemes where the amount contributed by the employee is a fixed proportion of his salary. This is matched by a similar contribution from the employer. The permutations are many.

According to the Government Actuary's last survey about 25 per cent of pensioners in occupational schemes receive a pension of £1 per week or less. Another 25 per cent receive between £1 and £2 per week. Only about one in four receives £5 a week or more. Most schemes are thus currently providing very modest pensions.

Most pension schemes contain separate provisions for different kinds of withdrawal benefit. Where members withdraw voluntarily, usually to take another job, they are normally entitled to receive their own accrued contributions together with interest. In some schemes the employee is entitled to take a "paid up" policy for a reduced pension payable at normal retirement age. This entitles the employee to the benefits secured by that time not only by his own contributions but by the contributions of his employer. Members who leave of their own free will are often granted the same benefits as those dismissed for redundancy, except that fewer of them receive the benefits of the employer's contributions. Even fewer still of the employees dismissed for some fault or other receive the benefits of the employer's contributions. About 30 per cent of all members of occupational pension schemes in the private sector are in schemes which provide for no preservation on voluntary withdrawal. About 40 per cent are in schemes which provide preservation at the employer's option, 20 per cent at the member's option and 10 per cent provide preservation in all cases. Only about one-quarter of private sector pension schemes have provision for accepting transfer values from other schemes. They cover, however, about one-half of the members of private schemes.

Within the public service and nationalised industries, arrangements for the transfer of pension rights on a change of employment are more common; in these schemes also the employer's agreement usually has to be obtained—although it is generally easier to get. The transfer value of the pension right does not, however, always take into account the full value of both the employee's and the employer's contributions. There has now grown up a patchwork of bilateral and illogical deals for transferring benefits between big pension funds and a network of arrangements between the civil service and the public corporations or quasi-public employment. Certain similar agreements operate for transfer between local government service and other public employment.

Despite the fact that the majority of members of occupational pension schemes now have *some* rights for the preservation of pension entitlement on change of employment it does not follow that when members actually change their employment preservation takes place. There are two principal reasons for this. Firstly, the rules of many pension schemes provide for preservation only at the discretion of the employer. Secondly, experience has shown beyond any shadow of doubt, that the majority of employees who change their employment prefer to exercise their option for the return of their own contributions as an alternative to preservation.

The report of the National Joint Advisory Council on *Preservation of Pension Rights* said that in 1963 some 39 per cent of all withdrawing employees had the opportunity to elect for some form of preservation but that in practice only one in five chose to do so. Of the employees who were dismissed—about 4 per cent of the total—over 50 per cent could have had their pension rights preserved, but only about one in four opted for this. Of those who withdrew voluntarily, about 37 per cent were offered some degree of preservation, but only about one in five of them opted for preservation. Of all withdrawing employees about 5 per cent had their pension rights fully or partially preserved by deferred pensions and something over 2 per cent benefited from the payment of a transfer value to a new employer.

The last report of the Government Actuary expressed the same conclusion. It said that in 1963 about 7 per cent of pensionable employees changed their jobs but only about one in ten of them had their pension rights preserved, apart from the preservation of National Insurance graduated pension. The proportion preserved was higher for dismissals than for voluntary withdrawals, and higher for those with long service than for those with short service. About one-half of all leavers were offered some form of preservation, but the majority preferred a refund of personal contributions.

There appear to be a number of reasons why employees prefer to have a refund of contributions than to avail themselves of preservation rights. The first is that many of them, particularly younger employees, welcome the opportunity to receive some ready cash. Pension rights do not, in the majority of cases, begin to assume importance until employees are over the age of, say, 35–40. Secondly, with continuing inflation and the depreciation of money, every £1 received now is substantially more valuable than when due as a pension many years ahead. This depreciation may be sufficient to offset not only the value of the employer's contributions which are forfeited when the employee withdraws his contributions but also the benefit of accrued interest payments. Thirdly, there is in many human beings an element of optimism or irresponsibility, however it may be described, which leads them to believe or to hope that "the future will look after itself".

The report of the National Joint Advisory Council rightly pointed out that if the right of employees to withdraw their contributions on a change of employment were to be preserved the whole purpose of introducing arrangements for the preservation of pension rights would be frustrated. The report said:

> The case for withdrawing the right to a return of contributions is in essence simple. The role of pension schemes is to provide benefits in retirement. If the right is to remain, the loss of benefits in retirement will be considerable and it must be doubted whether any general arrangements for preservation would have any significant effect. If it is accepted that preservation is desirable in as full terms as might be possible on general grounds of social policy, the continued existence of the right to a return of contributions once a qualification for preservation has been satisfied would almost entirely frustrate this objective. We have therefore concluded that the return of contributions in cash should not in general be permitted under arrangements for preservation. The rules of pension schemes would, however, have to provide for the return of an employee's own contributions in cases where qualifications for preservation had not been satisfied.

The report made one important exception to the general recommendation that the right to withdraw contributions should be ended. It said:

> We have found it necessary to consider whether any exceptions should be allowed from this condition. We have already pointed out that the great majority of women set particular value on the return of their contributions on withdrawal on or after marriage. Many women in such circumstances clearly contemplate relying on the provision which their husbands are making for retirement and the pension rights which married women have accumulated by withdrawal will in many cases be small and might well be seriously eroded over, say, a 30-year period to retirement. At the least, the withdrawal of their right to a return of contributions in cash would be widely unpopular and might serve no useful purpose. We consider it important that women should have the same rights to

preservation as other employees, but we nevertheless have concluded that an option for married women to the return of their contributions should remain as an alternative, although we recognise that a similar option is not given under the Graduated Pension Scheme.

The way in which National Insurance and private pension schemes have developed in Britain has created immense inequalities. Two citizens who have made a similar contribution to society throughout their working lives and who may have received similar incomes may find themselves at the age of 65 with very dissimilar pension entitlements. Indeed, material inequalities in old age have become greater than those which exist in working life. About a half of the working population can expect to retire on a State pension plus an occupational pension which, at the very least, will be better than the State graduated pension. The other half of the working population can expect nothing more than whatever is provided under the State scheme. If this inequality is to be reduced two things are essential. First, all workpeople should be able to earn a pension of at least half-pay as a return for their lifetime of work, Secondly, the right to a satisfactory pension ought not to be affected by changes of employment which are often to the direct benefit of the community.

If everything could be started afresh the rational way to achieve these objectives would be to make all pensions—as a return for a lifetime of labour—payable by the State. Contributions and benefits could be related to earnings and a great new tool for investment planning would be available. Such a radical change, however, is not possible quickly. Millions of people now have rights and expectations in existing private schemes and they, reasonably enough, will demand their rights. The only practicable course is to provide a State wage-related benefit scheme with generous terms for all who are not satisfactorily covered by private schemes. All private schemes should, however, offer benefits at least equal to those provided in the State scheme and should include arrangements for full transferability on change of employment.

Why this Expansion?

There have been four main reasons for the rapid development
in recent years of private occupational pension schemes. The
first is the understandable desire of employers to reduce labour
turnover, particularly among their highly skilled and specialist
staff. Thus an employee with a number of years' service is much
more reluctant to change his employment—even though a more
favourable wage may be offered to him—if he knows that he will
be sacrificing his ultimate pension. Moreover, firms which offer
a pension are in a stronger position to attract new labour. This
advantage is obviously eroded with the extension of pension
schemes to more and more firms. Ultimately, as is already the case
in some types of white collar employment, the firm without a
pension scheme will be the exception. When this stage is reached
private pension schemes tend to lose their advantage as a means
of attracting labour. Their main effect is to impede the mobility
of labour. We assert this based upon our own experience and are
not persuaded by the Report of the Committee of the National
Joint Advisory Council on *Preservation of Pension Rights* in 1966
which thought this argument was not "compelling".

The second main reason for the development of private pension
schemes is that some employers regard them as a means of discipline to prevent labour disputes. Workers who feel that their
pension rights may be threatened in an industrial dispute about
wages or conditions are likely to be reluctant to withdraw their
labour. Some employers will, of course, deny that they had motives of this kind when introducing a pension scheme. They may
be sincere. There are other employers who have not hesitated
to threaten the pension rights of their employees when they felt
it could help their purpose in an industrial dispute.

An interesting example of a firm's threat to pension rights in
an industrial dispute was provided in a dispute between Vickers-
Armstrongs (Shipbuilders) Ltd. and the Draughtsmen's and Allied
Technicians' Association in 1964. The dispute was about wages.
The Association submitted a wage claim on behalf of its members

employed at Vickers-Armstrongs, Barrow. The claim was taken through all stages of the negotiating arrangements between the Shipbuilding Employers' Federation and DATA. These negotiations did not lead to a settlement and the Association's members went on strike after giving proper notice to the firm. The strike was supported officially by the Association.

After the strike had been in progress for some weeks, the firm notified the strikers that unless they returned to work by a given date their employment would be terminated and their membership of the firm's pension scheme discontinued. They also stated that if at a later date following the ending of the strike the strikers were taken back into employment they would be required to re-enter the pension scheme. Because of the provisions of the Vickers' pension scheme—under which pensions are calculated by reference both to the length of service of the employee and his rate of pay in the final years of employment—the effect of the threat by the firm to the pension rights of the strikers would have been, if carried out, to have reduced the ultimate pension received by the draughtsmen who returned to work after the dispute was settled. DATA reacted very vigorously to this threat and extended the strike to Vickers-Armstrongs' establishment on Tyneside. They also alerted their members in the other main shipbuilding areas with a view to taking further action if the threat were not withdrawn.

At first the firm were supported by the Shipbuilding Employers' Federation. Later, however, it appeared that this support weakened. It may be that some of the other shipbuilding employers felt less than enthusiastic about supporting Vickers' authoritarian attitude. Their reluctance to give support might also have been strengthened by the obvious determination of other draughtsmen in the industry to join in the dispute if the threat were not withdrawn. The result of this strong stand by DATA was that the dispute was eventually settled satisfactorily and the threat to pension rights was withdrawn. The draughtsmen resumed work with their pension rights maintained.

The third main reason for the introduction of private pension schemes is that it enables employers to compel employees, who have reached the age of, say, 65 for men and 60 for women, to retire. If there were no pension scheme some employers, who show concern for the welfare of their workpeople, would be reluctant to dismiss long service employees, even though their efficiency had declined and their continued employment thwarted the promotion of younger and more energetic employees.

The fourth reason for the rapid development of private occupational pension schemes is the very favourable tax concessions which have been made for them. The Phillips Committee Report on the Economic and Financial Problems of the Provision for Old Age, 1954, pointed out that in 1936 there were estimated to be only about $1\frac{1}{2}$ million workers in industry and commerce covered by superannuation schemes. This figure, according to the Phillips Committee, had been trebled in less than 20 years. Employers are able to gain for themselves the advantages of occupational pension schemes with the assistance of what is, in effect, a substantial subsidy from the Exchequer.

In the year 1964/5 it was estimated that tax reliefs on occupational pension schemes amounted to about £65 million for employees, about £5 million for the self-employed and about £35 million for the investment income of superannuation funds. If employers' contributions to these schemes had not been deductable in computing business profits the additional tax payable for 1964/5 would have been about £160 million.

The Case for Transferability

The case for transferable pension rights when an employee changes his employment rests on the following main grounds:

(a) A pension is not a gratuity from an employer but deferred pay for service rendered. It is, therefore, unjust that this deferred pay should be surrendered by an employee when he changes his job. The NJAC Report acknowledges this argument in these words:

> The main reason put forward for the unfairness of pension arrangements which do not provide for preservation is that pensions are a form

of deferred pay and that employees should therefore be entitled to them as of right when they reach retirement age whether or not they are still in the same employment. There may not be general agreement that the right to a pension can be necessarily regarded as a right to deferred pay. We recognise however that as pension arrangements become more general, and to the extent to which their terms are negotiated with employees together with wages and other conditions of employment, it becomes understandable that the feeling should spread that pensions are a form of pay which is deferred until a later date.

(b) Non-transferable pensions impede the mobility of labour. Rigidity of this kind is not in the best long term interests of the nation. Over a period of years some sections of industry are bound to decline and others to expand. A corresponding flow of labour from the declining to the expanding industries is essential if the necessary adjustments are to be made quickly and with the least amount of hardship. Similarly, in certain kinds of employment it is desirable, that employees particularly when they are young, should change their job periodically in order to broaden their experience. Non-transferable pensions discourage employees from changing from one firm to another.

(c) The dismissal of a long-service employee for a misdemeanour may, if it results in the loss of pension rights, impose a penalty out of all proportion to the wrong which the employee has committed.

(d) Non-transferable pension schemes prejudice the employees' freedom of trade union action. If a union finds it necessary to exert pressure on an employer in support of a claim on wages or conditions an employee who is a member of a non-transferable pension scheme may be reluctant to take action because of the fear that his employer may attack his expected pension.

Transferability—Official Statements

Almost every authoritative investigation of the problem of non-transferable occupational pensions has led to the conclusion that transferability would be of economic advantage. The first report of the National Advisory Committee on the Employment of Older Men and Women (Command 8963, 1953) stated:

> The effect of pension schemes on the mobility of labour concerns us only in so far as it limits the opportunity for workers to transfer, if the need arises, to other employment as they become older. Under the National Insurance scheme no transfer difficulties arise; and in the public service, including for this purpose the nationalised industries, arrangements have been made to provide under certain conditions for the interchange of superannuation rights. But in private industry, although some schemes provide for such reciprocal arrangements, they are as yet a small minority. In practice, even if transfer rules did operate, they could only do so where the workers moved from one pensionable job to another pensionable job in schemes approved by the Inland Revenue and where the transfer of rights was agreed by those in control of the two schemes. In most pension schemes a withdrawing employee has the right to a paid-up pension corresponding to the actuarial value of his own contributions; but he usually forfeits that part of his prospective pension that is being provided by the employer's contribution. If accrued pension rights will be lost on leaving a particular employment there will naturally be reluctance to move even if this would be otherwise in the interests of the worker and of the work.

The Federation of British Industries in its evidence to the Millard–Tucker Committee on Taxation declared:

> It is desirable to facilitate the transfer of retirement benefit on a change of employment, both to avoid the loss of years of service during which retirement benefits can be built up and to avoid employees clinging to unsuitable employment to retain the accrued pension rights.

In 1954 the Phillips Committee on the Economic and Financial Problems of the Provision for Old Age (Command 9333) also reported on the advantage of transfer arrangements. Paragraph 248 of their report stated:

> In our view, arrangements whereby the accrued pension rights of a person with substantial service may be preserved on a change of employment, including movement between the public services and private employment, are in the general national interest and would facilitate the employment of older persons to which the National Advisory Committee has directed attention.

The Phillips Committee said that they had given much consideration to the suggestion that it should be made a condition of approval or recognition by the Commissioners of Inland Revenue that schemes should include provisions to ensure that if an employee who has reached a particular age, such as 40, or completed a specific number of years of pensionable employment, transfers to another employment with an approved scheme, a transfer value should pass, or, alternatively, where there is no approved scheme in the new employment the employee should be entitled to a paid up pension placed in "cold storage". The Committee stated that they had reluctantly concluded that although the practice of granting transfer values and particularly of granting paid up pensions to employees leaving an employment was spreading the general climate of opinion at that time was not such that compulsion should be used. Nevertheless, the Committee said, with the continued growth of pension schemes the time might not be far distant when the idea of general transferability or the provision of paid up pensions would come to be widely acceptable. The Committee went on to record their general approval of the growing practice of adopting methods to ensure the preservation of accrued pension rights.

In 1958 Government approval of the idea of transferable pension rights was contained in the "Statement on Provisions for Old Age" presented to Parliament by the Minister of Pensions and National Insurance. Paragraph 20 of this statement noted that there had been increasing movement, both in industry and in professional insurance circles, towards the idea that pension rights in occupational schemes should not be lost on change of employment. It was important from the national point of view, said the statement, that occupational pension schemes should not prevent "that degree of mobility of labour and equitable treatment on change of work which is needed in a healthy and expanding economy". The statement added that it was also desirable that contributions set aside for an individual's old age should remain saved for that object and should not be dissipated on a change of employment.

In 1963 the National Economic Development Council in their report on "Conditions Favourable to Faster Growth" referred to the possible loss by employees of their occupational pension rights when changing jobs as a factor impeding the necessary mobility of labour.

They said: "Consideration should be given to making preservation of pension rights on transfer of employment a condition of approval of a pension scheme by the Inland Revenue."

Finally, the National Joint Advisory Council report on the "Preservation of Pension Rights", published in 1966 said: ". . . the present position leaves an appreciable gap in the total provision for retirement and we believe on general grounds of social policy that effective arrangements for preservation are desirable."

The NJAC Report summarised the following possibilities:

   (i) Direct compulsion.

   (ii) The refusal of a deduction from taxable profits in respect of employers' contributions if an acceptable degree of preservation is not provided.

   (iii) The withholding of all tax reliefs from pension arrangements now available following approval by the Inland Revenue if an acceptable degree of preservation is not provided.

   (iv) The withholding of reliefs now available on Revenue approval together with the refusal of a deduction from taxable profits in respect of employers' contributions, if an acceptable degree of preservation is not provided.

   (v) The withholding of relief from the investment income of pension funds if an acceptable degree of preservation is not provided.

The NJAC Report did not feel able to recommend any particular method but they pointed out that exhortation alone, coupled with action by the Government in the public sector, would not be effective.

The report also stated that a system of tax incentives would neither be acceptable nor have the desired effect. It suggested that the imposition of a direct compulsory requirement on pension arrangements to provide for preservation "merits consideration". No method, it was pointed out, could provide a perfect solution free from all difficulties but the *minimum* aim should be the provision of deferred pensions on withdrawal. A qualifying condition would be essential before preservation could be required in respect of an individual employee and the report suggested either a service or an age and membership qualification. This qualification would be necessary because the preservation of trivial pensions would be uneconomic. The report also urged that preservation should be available as a right whatever the reason for an employee's withdrawal from a pension scheme.

The technical problems of providing a satisfactory national scheme for the preservation of pension rights require for their solution a detailed and intimate knowledge of taxation and insurance practice. There is, however, no reason to think that these problems are insurmountable. On 10 November 1965 the Minister of Labour, Mr. Ray Gunter, said, for example, at a conference of the National Association of Pension Funds:

> In the general debate on the question of preservation, a great deal of attention has been given to the technical and other difficulties inherent in the problem. These are very real. They arise from the many different forms pension arrangements can take, the various ways in which these can be financed, differences in rules and the benefits they provide and their place in the tax system. I have no intention of reviewing these difficulties in detail. Many of them are clearly the province of experts. But I am certain that these difficulties can and will be surmounted.

The cost of introducing preservation by deferred pensions for all employees was estimated by the NJAC report at £50 million a year, although, they pointed out, "this figure would be reduced in practice by the imposition of qualifications for preservation...". The additional cost would be equivalent to about 5 per cent of the total contributions to pension arrangements or about 0·5 per cent of the total wages and salaries of members of existing schemes.

Apart from the pension schemes in public employment, including the nationalised industries, the Phillips Committee drew attention to two other large superannuation schemes where provision is made for transferable pensions between firms in the same industry. The two schemes were for employees in the flour-milling industry and for officers in the Merchant Navy. An employee who transfers from one firm to another in either of these schemes carries his accrued rights with him and the need for the passage of transfer values or the provision of "cold storage" pensions does not arise.

A pamphlet entitled *Protect Your Pension*, written by Mr. John Fryd, the General Secretary of the National Federation of

Professional Workers, referred to two other schemes which provide for transferable pensions for changes of employment within the same occupation. They are the solicitors' law clerks scheme and the Social Workers' Pension Fund. This second scheme covers employers in a wide variety of voluntary organisations.

Other Countries

Both the Phillips Report and the NJAC reports pointed out that arrangements for transferable pensions exist in a number of other countries where occupational pension schemes are firmly established.

In the Netherlands a law of 1954 stipulates strict conditions for pension funds. A pension fund cannot exist unless it has been approved under the 1954 Act. The rules of pension funds must provide for the preservation of accrued pension rights, based on both the employer's and the employee's contributions, of all members withdrawing after more than 5 years' membership. Preservation, said the NJAC Report, is always effected by the award of a deferred pension and the rules must not allow the payment of a lump sum in respect of these rights unless this would only be a very small amount, or unless a female member is withdrawing because of marriage, or unless the employee is emigrating. Full transferability is provided between public employments, and, in practice, the Government conform to the requirements of the 1954 Act on changes of employment between the public and private sectors.

In Canada voluntary private pension provision often supplements Federal pension schemes. Many private schemes have maintained rules recommended by a former Federal Income Tax Code of Practice which called for vesting of accrued pension rights in an employee who left after the age of 50 with at least 20 years' service. Ontario has introduced legislation requiring full vesting of the accrued pension rights for employees leaving over age 45 and with at least 10 years' service. An employee who meets these conditions cannot withdraw his own contributions except, if the rules of the scheme allow, a cash sum equal in value to not more than 25 per cent of the pension benefits.

In Denmark there are few occupational pension schemes for manual workers but there are extensive schemes for salaried workers. One such scheme is operated by a large private pensions organisation, formed in 1917 by employers' organisations, and accounts for more than half the total industrial pensions business. The unions are represented in the management of this scheme. The principle of transferable pension rights is universally established not only within the one large scheme but between all existing schemes. The Danish Insurance Board, established by law, requires companies to provide for the transfer of pension business when employees change their jobs. Under most schemes in Denmark the employee is not entitled to exercise an option for a refund of contributions when he changes employment. The only exceptions are when an employee emigrates or when a female employee marries.

In France there is widespread provision for contributory occupational pension schemes to supplement State schemes. Benefits are provided through a number of industry wide funds linked together by compensation agreements. Pension rights are generally preserved on change of employment.

In Norway the system is similar in some respects to that in Denmark. Provision is normally made for the preservation of occupational pension rights on change of employment. The largest scheme in industry was established by the employers and unions and is conducted as an allied service by the national insurance administration.

In Sweden transfer arrangements exist for staff employees in private industry through a jointly owned union–employer company. A Swedish union replied to an inquiry from the authors of this book in these words:

> We have formed a special company (Swedish Staff Pensioning Society —SPP) handling the pensions owned by industries and unions. The employer has to pay a certain percentage of the employee's salary to this company, and it gives the employee complete independence and he can

choose to stay on or leave and take up a new employment without this interfering with his pension rights. The only thing he has to do is to make sure that his new employer agrees to take the SPP. If the employer refuses to do that the union moves in and can take any steps needed forcing the employer to agree to this thing. We can in this case put on a strike if the employer refuses to pay.

Political Parties—Their Policies

A brief statement of the attitude of the three political parties, Conservative, Labour and Liberal, to transfer arrangements for occupational pension schemes was set out in replies to an inquiry made by the National Federation of Professional Workers in the summer of 1964. The inquiry was made as a result of a resolution on the subject adopted by the Federation at its 1964 annual conference.*

Viscount Blakenham replied on behalf of the Conservative Party. He said that the Party regarded the development of a greater degree of preservation of rights in private pension schemes on change of employment as a matter of major importance. As, however, there was no legal obligation on an employer to provide a pension scheme at all, the Party did not think that compulsion was the best method of securing transfer arrangements.

Viscount Blakenham claimed that the Conservative Party had already given a considerable impetus to the development of preservation of pension rights by making preservation, in one way or another, of pensions up to the maximum of the State graduated scheme a condition of contracting out under the National Insurance Act, 1959. He added that employers should be encouraged to develop preservation in their schemes and the Conservative Party would do all that it could to help.

* The NFPW has an affiliated membership of more than 1 million salaried employees in trade unions in the public services and in private industry and commerce. Unions representing some of the performers and staff in the entertainment industry are also affiliated to the Federation. The NFPW has good relations with the TUC and many of its affiliated organisations are also affiliated to the TUC.

In his reply on behalf of the Labour Party Mr. Harold Wilson (before he became Prime Minister) stated that his Party had been concerned for some time at the way in which the non-transferability of private pension schemes stood in the way of adequate labour mobility essential for an expanding economy. The size of the problem could be seen from the fact that, according to Professor Titmuss, between 1957 and 1960 no less than 1,143,000 people had to forfeit their pension rights because they changed their job and there was non-transferability of pension rights. Because of this, said Mr. Wilson, the Labour Party had outlined its plans in April 1963 in *New Frontiers for Social Security*. The Party intended to enforce transferability of pension rights in private schemes.

The reply from the Liberal Party came from Mr. T. H. Emerson, the secretary to the Liberal Parliamentary Party. He said that the Liberals had taken the lead over the last few years in pressing for the preservation of pension rights on transfer of employment. He referred to an amendment to the Finance Bill to provide for the preservation of pension rights which had been moved by Mr. Donald Wade, the Liberal Member of Parliament. The amendment moved by Mr. Wade was as follows:

(1) In section 379 of the Income Tax Act 1952 (Approved superannuation funds), in subsection (3) there shall be added the following paragraph:

"(e) the rules of the fund provide that an employee who leaves the employment of an employer in the trade or undertaking for reasons other than fraud or misconduct by the employee shall not thereby be deprived of the benefits provided for him in the fund."

(2) In section 388 of the Income Tax Act 1952 (Approval of retirement benefits schemes), in subsection (1) there shall be added the following:

"(g) that the rules of the scheme provide that a person who leaves the employment of his employer for reasons other than fraud or misconduct by that person shall not thereby be deprived of the benefits provided for him in the scheme."

At the 1964 General Election the Labour Party promised to implement a Charter of Rights for all employees. This would include, the Party said, "the right to full transferability of pension entitlements". In its 1966 General Election manifesto the Labour

Party said: "We shall . . . . deal with the problem of transferability of occupational pensions."

In the statement of Conservative aims, *Putting Britain Right Ahead*, published in the autumn of 1965, the Party said:

> Nearly two-thirds of the adult male working population are already in occupational pension schemes. We believe that an arrangement should be made for all to be covered by occupational or similar pensions on top of the State basic pension. These schemes would have to meet specified minimum standards—including some provision for widows. And, as we have already said, we would insist on the transferability or preservation of occupational pension rights.

In the 1966 General Election the manifesto of the Conservative Party stated that the Party would: "Ensure that everyone can either transfer or preserve their pension when they change jobs."

The 1966 General Election manifesto of the Liberal Party said: ". . . and pension rights must be fully transferable."

Pensions and the National Interest

Once it is accepted that transfer arrangements in occupational pension schemes are in the national interest as well as being in the personal interest of individual employees there is no reason why pension schemes should not be made to conform to the national interest. It was the Phillips Committee which pointed out: "A substantial proportion of the cost of occupational pension schemes is borne by the Exchequer by way of tax relief. We consider, therefore, that it is reasonable to require that, in general, the schemes should not conflict with national policy."

Provision for transfer arrangements should be made a condition of approval or recognition by the Commissioners of Inland Revenue.

The National Federation of Professional Workers, in urging that legislation should be introduced for transfer arrangements in occupational pension schemes, suggested that there might be four ways in which the full benefit earned by both employee and employer contributions to an occupational pension scheme could be preserved.* The first was by the merging of individual firms' pension schemes into group, industry or service schemes, enabling pension rights to be maintained without any transfer of funds when employees move from one firm to another within the group, industry or service. The second was by the transfer of funds to an approved pension scheme in the new employment, with credit being given for the years of membership in the previous pension scheme. This method, the NFPW pointed out, requires that the schemes, whether contributory or not, should be to some degree comparable as to benefits. The third was by transferring the accrued actuarial value of the member's rights from the scheme covering his former employment to the scheme covering his new employment. The fourth was to provide the employee who changes his job with a paid-up policy for a pension to be drawn from the normal date of retirement. This method could be used when, for one reason or other, all other methods are unsuitable or impracticable. The NFPW pointed out, however, that it is the method least likely to encourage the new employer to agree to any adjustment to meet inflation or to relate the final pension to the total years of employment as well as to the final salary. Moreover, if an employee finds at the end of his working life that because of changes of employment he has acquired a number of paid up policies his total pension will reflect not his final salary but the average of his salary throughout his period of employment. From the employees' point of view, therefore, this method of preserving pension rights is not usually so advantageous as the other methods.

In addition to providing for the preservation of occupational pension rights any new legislation ought to prohibit the repayment of contributions on change of employment. The purpose of a pension scheme is to provide a pension; not to provide a capital grant on change of employment.

It will be seen that the subject has been much investigated but positive action remains to be taken: reform is still over the horizon.

* See *Protect Your Pensions* by John Fryd, General Secretary, National Federation of Professional Workers.

A majority of workers (mainly manual employees) are still outside of occupational pension schemes: *their* employers do not provide this benefit.

For those who *are* covered there are snags too. The field is well, even abundantly researched. Cannot the Government move on this?

CHAPTER 7

How long a work week ? How long to rest ? A minimum wage ?

IT HAS been widely accepted in the British trade union movement that except in special circumstances minimum labour standards relating to hours of work, holidays with pay and minimum rates should be determined by collective bargaining and not by legislation. Industry, it is said, should be encouraged to "govern itself". The responsibility for reaching agreement on working conditions should be placed squarely on the shoulders of the employers' and workers' organisations. Through the process of collective bargaining the negotiators will then be able to take account of the peculiarities of the industry in which they are engaged and arrangements can be settled which suit the needs of each particular occupation of industry. So the traditional nostrum runs, or did until the Prices and Incomes Act which was swallowed with hardly any visible straining.

Collective Bargaining and Legislation

There are certainly strong and even unanswerable arguments for collective bargaining in any kind of industrial and commercial society, whether under public or private ownership. But they are not necessarily arguments against the establishment of certain *minimum* standards by legislation. Similarly, the conclusion of voluntary national agreements by collective bargaining for minimum rates and conditions does not necessarily preclude local bargaining for better conditions based on factors related to a particular factory or locality.

The case for putting a level floor under the bargainers is unaffected by whether the floor rests on other bargains or a law. Improvements in working conditions can and have been obtained both by collective bargaining *and* by legislation .The one does not exclude the other. British industrial history during the last 150 years provides many examples of this dual push for improvements.

There have been periods, of course, when the main energies of the trade unions and the wider labour movement have been directed in one or the other direction, when different methods have been in fine focus. In fact, however, if there is any lesson it is that the struggle for better conditions must be conducted on all fronts. Trade unionism expressed through collective bargaining and industrial action, though an extremely potent influence, is not by itself always sufficient. It needs to be supplemented by political action aimed, among other objectives, at securing legislation for minimum labour standards.

In Britain the trend is towards more legislative provision for minimum labour standards. It is, however, a fairly slow trend. Many employers retard it because of their reluctance, particularly among their more backward number (big and small, for political as well as economic reasons), to accept improvements in minimum conditions and because of their opposition to almost any extension of statutory regulations affecting the conduct of their undertakings—and qualifying their almost mystical "managerial rights". The unions have sometimes dragged their feet because of their suspicion that legislation might prejudice collective bargaining or impose obligations which they might find onerous. Some unions have no appetite for gains. Some behave as if things were so good already that they may be tapped on the shoulder and told "give it back: it's all a mistake". Nevertheless, in some respects, the unions have set the pace in the demand for new legislation in relation to the health, welfare and safety of workers in their employment: but they certainly could and should have done more.

Comparison

There might be more to be said in favour of this oddly wide-spread British reluctance to establish minimum labour standards by legislation if it could be shown that the improvements in working conditions in Britain in recent years compared favourably with those secured in most other industrial countries. It could then be said that the British method had produced the results to justify its retention without significant alteration. The facts do not support any such complacent conclusion. On the contrary, protective labour standards in Britain have improved at a some-what slower pace in recent years than in many other countries. This is not to say that labour standards in Britain have fallen *drastically* behind. But, in some respects, they are not today up to good international practice and not enough people seem to have noticed this. This is certainly true in relation to hours of work and holidays.

In a number of countries the average hours of work in industry are fewer than in Britain. Unfortunately, however, because of differences in definition and differences in the scope of the figures between various countries it is not possible to compile a simple comparative table from figures published in the *ILO Year Book of Statistics*.

In November 1964 the *Ministry of Labour Gazette* published a table of average hours worked per week for workers in Belgium, France, Western Germany, Italy, Netherlands and Sweden. The figures related to 1963. Regrettably, no similar table has since been published in the *Ministry of Labour Gazette*. The table was as shown in Table 1 on page 122.

In October 1963 in Britain the average hours worked by adult male manual workers in a wide range of manufacturing industries and services were 47·6 per week. For manufacturing industry alone the average hours worked were 46·8. For women over 18 years of age the equivalent figures were 39·7 hours and 39·6 hours per week.

The figures given in the *ILO Year Book of Statistics* show that since 1963 there has been a general trend towards shorter working

TABLE 1

	1963 Average hours worked per week
BELGIUM	
All manufacturing	not available
Engineering	39·6
Chemicals	40·9
Textiles	40·4
FRANCE[a]	
All manufacturing (inc. building)	46·7
WESTERN GERMANY	
All manufacturing	44·4
ITALY	
All manufacturing	37·3
NETHERLANDS[b]	
All manufacturing	47·2
SWEDEN[b]	
All manufacturing	38·5

[a] Includes salaried employees.

[b] Adult male workers.

hours. The comparative position, however, outlined in the Ministry of Labour table does not, nevertheless, appear to have changed significantly.

The latest figures for Britain show that in the second pay week in October 1966 average hours worked by adult male manual workers in a wide range of manufacturing industries and services were 46·0 per week. For manufacturing industry alone the average hours worked were 45·0. For women over 18 years of age the equivalent figures were 38·1 and 38·0 hours per week.

The following figures were taken from a table on hours of

work in manufacturing industries published in the January–February 1967 issue of the *Economic and Social Bulletin of the International Confederation of Free Trade Unions.*

	1965		1965
Austria[a]	43·4	Ireland	43·9
France	45·6	Norway[a, b]	38·3
Germany (Federal Republic)	44·1	Switzerland	44·9
Great Britain[b]	46·1		

[a] Including mining and quarrying.
[b] Adult males only.

Again, because of the differences in the cover of the statistics, these figures have to be taken with reserve. They confirm, nevertheless, that Britain is not way ahead of other countries.

For some other countries outside western Europe, including the United States, the USSR, Canada, Australia and New Zealand the comparison is even less favourable to Britain. In the USA, Canada, Australia and New Zealand a basic 40-hour week or less is the general industrial practice. In the USA there are important sections of industry, including the manufacture of ladies' garments in New York, printing, rubber, brewing, dock work, jewellery, millinery, furs, lumber, the film industry, distribution and the construction trades where substantial numbers of workers have a basic week of less than 40 hours. In the USA about 7 per cent of the hours worked in manufacturing industry are in addition to the basic working week. Average hours worked are certainly less than in British industry.

In the USSR it was claimed that by January 1963 the average hours of work for all wage-earners were 39·4 per week and 40 hours in industry alone. A 35-hour week is already being observed in certain arduous occupations. A further shortening of the working week is also to take place over a fairly long period with the aim of achieving eventually a 35-hour week for most workers and a 30-hour week for those engaged in specially arduous occupations. In the spring of 1967, on the other hand, the Soviet Union announced that it was to introduce a 5-day working week of 41 hours. This was announced as a step forward because previously the working week had been spread over six days. It is difficult to reconcile the 41-hour working week with the average hours worked in 1963.

A basic 40-hour week for industrial workers has also been established in Indonesia. In France the basic working week of 40 hours was introduced in 1936 in all industrial and commercial establishments but the intention of the Act has, unfortunately, been undermined by widespread and persistent overtime. A basic 40-hour week has also been established by collective agreements in a number of industries in Germany. An agreement there for a 40-hour week in engineering, for example, preceded a similar agreement for a 40-hour week in the British engineering industry and was used to great effect in securing the 40-hour week in British shipbuilding. Ted Hill, the Boilermakers' negotiator, insisted he would not take less than the Germans and this was a key factor in establishing the first beach head. But we were very late.

Holidays

The comparison between Britain and other countries in respect of holidays is even less favourable to Britain. Workers in most industrial European countries enjoy more holidays each year than British workers. The ILO report *Annual Holidays with Pay*, 1964, revealed that of 92 States examined only 23 had a minimum holiday of less than 2 weeks (excluding public holidays). Forty-one States prescribed a minimum holiday of from 12 to 15 working days—and for two of these a higher minimum existed for part of the working population—and 27 had determined a minimum holiday of 3–4 weeks. The ILO report stressed that the information which it had given related to the *minimum* length of holiday and that in practice the duration of holidays were often longer for a substantial number of workers.

These longer holidays are usually prescribed by collective agreement or other joint machinery and often have been in existence for a long time. They occur even in the countries—for example France—where the legal holidays are already longer than the normal length of holiday received by British workers. In France the legal minimum annual holiday is 18 working days rising to a minimum 20 working days after 20 years' service, 22 working days after 25 years' service and 24 working days after 30 years' service. Young persons under 18 years of age are also entitled to a minimum holiday of 24 working days. The number of days of public holiday in France, received in addition to the annual holidays, is 11. Most industries in France covered by collective agreements, particularly those in manufacturing, now have a four-week annual holiday. This is a good illustration of the fusion of legislative and collective bargaining action to produce longer holidays.

The number of countries which provide for a minimum length of holidays by legislation has increased very considerably in recent years. The ILO report *Annual Holidays With Pay* stated:

> On the national level the vast increase in the number of countries having statutory holiday requirements demonstrates a clear trend towards increasing recognition of legislation or regulations as the most appropriate means of determining minimum annual leave.

At the same time the report stressed that though minimum holiday standards are laid down by law in many countries, the importance of collective agreements should not be underestimated. Collective agreements provide a means of improving holiday standards beyond the statutory minimum and also provide a means for ensuring that statutory requirements are observed for a policing action. Moreover, collective agreements provide, as the ILO report pointed out, "a means of ensuring the necessary flexibility in this constantly moving and progressing field". Parliaments cannot be expected to monitor and rectify with the precision desired in this area.

Of countries with a minimum annual holiday longer than the

2 weeks which is customary for many manual workers in
Britain the ILO report lists the following

MINIMUM DURATION OF BASIC ANNUAL HOLIDAYS

14 working days	Bulgaria, Yugoslavia
15 working days or 2 weeks plus 3 days	Colombia, Federal Republic of Germany, Luxembourg (non-manual), Netherlands (collective agreements), Philippines (public sector and certain collective agreements)
18 working days, or 3 weeks	Australia, Cameroon, Central African Republic, Ceylon (certain trades), Chad, Congo (Brazzaville), Dahomey, Denmark, Finland, France, Gabon, Guinea, Iceland, Ivory Coast, Malagasy Republic, Mali, Mauritania, Morocco, Niger, Norway, Senegal, Switzerland (certain cantons), Togo, Upper Volta
20 working days	Brazil, Uruguay
24 working days, 4 weeks or 1 month	Cuba, Nicaragua, Peru, Sweden

The above minimum holidays refer in most cases to all workers.
In a few countries, however, agricultural workers are not included.
In Australia and Morocco, for example, agricultural workers are
entitled to 2 weeks instead of 3.

The ILO report also indicates that at the time of its preparation
a number of countries were contemplating measures, or had submitted proposals to their parliaments, with a view to introducing
new or improved legislation on holidays. They included Gilbert
and Ellice Islands, Grenada, Netherlands, Philippines, and
Switzerland for the introduction of minimum statutory holidays;
Byelorussia and Portugal for the lengthening of the duration of
annual holidays; Costa Rica, Cyprus, Czechoslovakia, Ethiopia,
Fiji, Iraq, Luxembourg, Malaysia (Sabah) and Turkey for the
improvement of the relevant standards or for revising holiday
legislation as a whole. In Britain there was no common approach
or even a recognition of its desirability.

The existing holiday arrangements in a number of other West
European industrial countries are as follows.

Belgium. In 1965, 18 working days' holiday became general. Young workers under 18 years of age and underground workers in coal mines normally receive longer holidays than the general minimum. For the 3 weeks' general minimum holiday workers receive 2 weeks at double the normal rate of pay and 1 week at normal wages. The number of statutory public holidays is 10 per year and there are 5 other "recognised" days of holiday. Legislative provision is made for payment for 10 days of public holiday. In practice, payment is made varying from 10 to 15 days.

German Federal Republic. The minimum length of holiday is stipulated by law. Fifteen working days are granted after 6 months' employment. Workers over 35 years of age receive 18 days' holiday. The legal minima are supplemented by collective agreements. Nearly 95 per cent of collective agreements provide for holidays of 15 working days or more, and of these 75 per cent provide for 19 days or more. The trend is to increase the number of days of holiday entitlement on grounds of age. Young persons under 18 years of age receive additional days' holiday. Disabled workers, victims of Nazi persecution, and workers in certain arduous occupations also receive additional days' holiday. The number of public holidays varies from one region to another according to the predominant religious belief of the area. Public holidays vary between 10 to 13 days.

Italy. The Constitution stipulates that all workers shall receive a paid annual holiday. The minimum length of holiday is laid down in legislation for certain categories of workers, but for most workers the minimum length of holiday is determined by collective agreement. The minimum length of holiday in collective agreements usually rises from 12 working days after 1 year's service to 14 working days after 5 years' service and 18 working days after 20 years' service. Apprentices are legally entitled to a minimum 30 working days' holiday up to the age of 16 and 20 working days from 16 to 20 years of age. The number of public holidays in Italy is exceptionally high. There are 17 days of public holiday for which payment is made at the normal time rate of wages. Foremen and salaried workers in Italy have a longer minimum holiday entitlement than most manual workers. Such workers with special responsibility have a minimum of 15 working days' holiday, rising to 20 days after 3 years' service, 25 days after 11 years and 29 days after 19 years' service. Salaried workers have 15 days' minimum holiday rising to 20 days after 2 years' service, 25 days after 10 years and 30 days after 18 years.

Netherlands. The minimum length of holiday is determined mainly by collective agreements. Legal provision is made for the small minority of workers who are not covered by collective agreements. The normal minimum holiday stipulated in collective agreements is 15 working days. An additional 2 or 3 days are granted to young workers and sometimes for length of service. A special feature of many Dutch collective agreements on holidays is the provision of double pay for either part or the whole of the holiday period. The number of recognised public holidays varies from 6 to 9 days each year.

Sweden. All workers must receive by law a minimum 4 weeks' holiday after 1 year's service. This provision was in full operation from 1965. Workers who are employed in occupations dangerous to health are entitled to longer holidays. The number of days of public holiday is 12 each year, together with 2 "recognised" half-days. Collective agreements normally provide for payment for 11 days to workers with more than 4 months' service.

Legislation

Britain is not totally without legislative provision for hours of work and holidays. The Minister of Labour may issue wage regulation Orders under the Wages Councils Act, 1959, and these Orders may specify minimum rates of pay for a basic working week of a certain length. The Order may also specify overtime rates. But these Orders usually apply in poorly organised industries where standards are low. There is no pattern-setting here. About $3\frac{1}{2}$ million workers are within the scope of Wages Councils established under the Act. Similar provision is also made for workers in agriculture under the Agricultural Wages Act, 1948, and the

Agricultural Wages (Scotland) Act, 1949. The Wages Councils Act, 1949, the Agricultural Wages Act, 1948, and the Agricultural Wages (Scotland) Act, 1949, also provide powers for the statutory fixing of holidays with pay.

Even as late as the second half of the 1930's the majority of employed persons in Britain receiving a wage or salary of less than £250 a year did not receive holidays with pay. In 1937 a Committee of Inquiry was appointed by the Minister of Labour to investigate how far paid holidays were provided in industry and how far their provision could be extended by statutory enactment or otherwise. The Committee, in a unanimous report, recommended that an annual holiday with pay equivalent to the working week should be established for all workers, and that every possible effort should be made to establish this holiday with pay by voluntary arrangement. They urged that the Minister of Labour should promote the adoption of voluntary agreements for paid holidays.

Another recommendation of the Committee was that statutory wage-fixing bodies should be empowered to consider and determine whether the provision of a holiday with pay should be granted. The Committee pronounced in favour of legislative provision for holidays with pay in industry generally. At the same time they made it clear that any legislation on holidays with pay should not adversely affect any more favourable provisions which might already exist.

The Government of the day accepted the recommendations of the Committee of Inquiry. In 1938 the Holidays with Pay Act was passed which empowered all statutory wage-fixing bodies to give directions for holidays with pay covering workers for whom they prescribed minimum wages. The further legislation, encouraged by the Committee of Inquiry, to provide holidays with pay for *all* workers in industry was never introduced. The Committee of Inquiry had suggested that it should be produced in the 1940/1 Parliamentary Session. In 1939, Britain entered the Second World War and discussion on proposals for legislation on holidays with pay was deferred until the post-war period.

TUC Policy

Rule 2 of the constitution of the TUC declares that one of the objects of Congress is to secure a legal maximum working week of 40 hours. During the 1930's the General Council of the TUC persistently argued that hours should be reduced from 47 or 48 to 40. Their efforts were unsuccessful: their arguments were rejected, although chronic unemployment existed.

In 1944 the General Council of the TUC circulated to all affiliated unions a statement on the history of the negotiations for a 40-hour week, together with proposals for securing the adoption of the 40-hour week at the end of the war. The General Council proposed that a direct request should be made to the British Government for legislation providing for a general reduction in the hours of labour to 40 per week. It was suggested that the legislation should be of a kind enabling the principle to be applied in each industry or section of industry according to its particular circumstances. Elasticity should be allowed, it was said, in the application of the standard, and the employers and unions should be empowered to arrange the detailed application of the 40-hour week to their industry.

The annual report of the TUC General Council for 1944 summarised the proposals for legislation. It said:

> The General Council feel that the Minister of Labour should be given power to recognise voluntary agreements in all industries regarding the application of the 40-hour week, and that in those industries where, either due to the opposition of the employers' association or the unorganised condition of the industry, a scheme for this reform fails to mature, the Minister should be empowered to require that a draft scheme should be submitted to him within a specified time. In the event of failure to secure such a draft scheme, the Minister should be responsible for drafting a scheme, after consultation with such bodies of workpeople and employers as he may be able to contact in the industry or section of industry concerned. In order to reinforce the Minister of Labour in this connection, it is suggested that the Bill should provide for the appointment of a Commission, representative of industry, which would have the responsibility of advising him whether or not the arrangements in an industry or section of an industry met with the requirements of the Bill (after it had become an Act) and if not, of recommending to him what he should do to bring it in line with the legislation.

The 1944 Congress carried a resolution supporting the General Council's request for legislation on the 40-hour week. The resolution also expressed the opinion that "two weeks' annual holiday with pay should also be provided for by legislation . . .".

Following the 1944 Congress the General Council set up a special committee to consider and to give advice on the further steps to be taken to implement the proposals of the TUC on the 40-hour week and holidays with pay. At the 1945 Congress the chairman of the special committee, Sir Mark Hodgson, introduced the appropriate paragraphs of the General Council's report. He explained that in some industries the 40-hour week might have to be introduced in stages. The practical way in one industry, he said, might not be the practical way in another.

> The aim must be a scheme in each industry providing for the 40 hour week at an early date, and in a manner according to the needs as ascertained as far as possible by joint examination, while a general stimulus is given by broad legislation providing for initiation of this reform.

Sir Mark Hodgson explained that a similar approach, both for legislative and voluntary action, would be made in relation to holidays with pay.

During 1945–6 the General Council sought to stimulate the activities of affiliated unions to secure a 40-hour week. Negotiations were conducted in a considerable number of industries, and discussions took place between the General Council and representatives of the Labour Party. The 1946 report of the General Council summarised the proposals for legislation advocated by the TUC. Legislation, it said, should be designed to give legal effect to arrangements for a 40-hour week arrived at by voluntary negotiation, and should impose on industries in which the voluntary method of approach was found to be unavailing an obligation to prepare a satisfactory scheme. If such a scheme were not drawn up the Minister of Labour should himself be empowered, with technical assistance and the advice of the specially appointed Commission, to draw up an appropriate scheme. The TUC also suggested that the proposed legislation should require statutory wage-fixing bodies to give immediate consideration to the implementation of the 40-hour week.

The General Council's report to the 1946 Congress recorded, as a principal modification of policy, that the TUC was now definitely prepared to see the 40-hour week established, where appropriate, in two stages. This was, however, subject to the qualification that in industries already working less than 47–48 hours there was no obvious reason why a 40-hour week or less should not be reached in one step.

The General Council's report also recorded that discussions had taken place with the Minister of Labour on holidays with pay. The report stated: "The Minister expressed his willingness sympathetically to consider the possibility of introducing legislation on holidays with pay at an early date if suitable legislation could be prepared in time."

The 1946 Congress approved the policy of the General Council on the 40-hour week and holidays with pay not only by accepting the General Council's report but also by adopting a motion on the subject moved by the Transport and General Workers' Union. This pledged support for efforts to establish a 40-hour week and 2 weeks' holiday with pay and urged the General Council to make immediate representations to the Government for legislation on lines previously advocated by the TUC.

This marked the high-point of the post-war campaign for legislation. By the following year the General Council reported to Congress that "a further approach to the Government by the Forty-hour Week Committee on the isolated problem of reduced hours of work would have been inappropriate". The General Council's report spoke of the difficulties which industry had undergone, including a fuel crisis, a severe winter and a drain on dollar credits. Nevertheless, the General Council were able to record that during the year many industries had secured appreciable reductions in their normal working week and that a very wide section of the economy was now based on normal hours of 44 or 45 per week. Other industries, the General Council said, were coming into line and thus the first stage of the

TUC programme towards a general 40-hour week was being secured.

The paragraphs of the General Council's report dealing with holidays with pay also pronounced in favour of a deferment of an approach to the Government for suitable legislation. In justification of this view the General Council's report referred to the difficulties arising from the economic crisis, to the need for increased production and to the introduction of a shorter working week in a number of industries. A motion on the 40-hour week which had been tabled for the 1947 Congress was withdrawn. The trade union movement had quickly run out of steam.

Some years were to pass before Congress was to return to the subject of the 40-hour week. At the 1948 Congress a motion asking that the Government should be urged to provide legislation for the introduction of 2 weeks' annual leave with pay for all workers was withdrawn on the understanding that it would be considered by the General Council. The following year the General Council reported that whilst note had been taken of the fact that it was Congress policy to favour legislation for 2 weeks' holiday with pay they (i.e. the General Council) "felt that in the prevailing economic situation legislation to provide this would be likely to have unfavourable repercussions". At the 1949 Congress a motion calling for certain changes in the rules and standing orders of the TUC was remitted to the General Council. The motion sought, among other matters, to amend one of the stated objects of the TUC relating to hours of labour. The existing rule called for a legal maximum working week of 44 hours. The remitted motion urged that this should be amended to "A legal maximum five-day working week of 40 hours". The following year, 1950, the General Council recommended that the rule should be amended to "A legal maximum working week of 40 hours". This was accepted by Congress.

In 1953 and 1954 the subject of holidays with pay was discussed at the conference of the ILO. A formal Recommendation was adopted. It was reported to the 1954 Congress of the TUC. The Recommendation, which applied to all workers with the exception of seafarers, agricultural workers and family undertakings, suggested a minimum annual holiday with pay of 2 working weeks for 12 months of service. It also suggested that in each country the appropriate machinery should determine whether the duration of the paid holiday should increase with length of service. The Recommendation also proposed that young persons under 18 years of age should receive a longer period of annual holiday than the proposed general minimum of 2 working weeks.

The 1954 Congress debated a motion, sponsored by the Blacksmiths' Society, calling for a drastic reduction in overtime and a vigorous campaign to achieve the 40-hour week. The General Council of the TUC were not prepared to support the motion because, as their spokesman put it, regular overtime in some sections of British industry was unavoidable. In their view, the General Council's spokesman said, it would be improper to evade that obligation. The General Council made it clear, however, that they regarded the 40-hour week as a general objective of the trade union movement.

The sponsors of the 40-hour week motion refused to accept the suggestion that it should be remitted to the General Council. Instead they pressed it to a vote. The General Council then urged that it should be rejected. The motion was defeated by 4,303,000 to 3,644,000. The vote was taken in a feverish atmosphere at the Congress and at one stage a violent argument took place in the miners' delegation. The National Union of Mineworkers cast their vote against the motion. One of the miners' delegates shouted for all to hear: "Mr. President, the miners' votes are a fiddle." A point of order was raised and eventually Mr. Ernest Jones, the miners' president, went to the rostrum to explain that, following a discussion which they had taken in 1949, it was the practice of the NUM to cast their vote in support of the General Council's point of view if and when a union sponsoring a motion did not agree to remit it. This extraordinary doctrine was decisive in defeating a very moderate reforming motion.

The following year the 40-hour week debate was repeated at the Congress. This time the Blacksmiths' Society sponsored a motion stating that the time was now opportune to achieve the 40-hour week. It was clear from the debate that many unions and delegates attached importance to reversing the defeat of the previous year. This time, moreover, the miners' delegation decided to support the motion and Mr. Abe Moffat, the Scottish miners' leader, spoke on their behalf.

The General Council this time asked for the motion to be withdrawn. Mr. Frank Cousins was their spokesman. He emphasised that the General Council did not oppose the principle of the 40-hour week. He went on:

> They [i.e. the General Council] do think that unions have a right to determine, in the light of the circumstances, what would be good for the particular trades they represent, but it is not fair to suggest to the members, particularly in organisations catering for general workers, that we are going willy-nilly, regardless of the consequences, to suggest that we should all go for a forty-hour week.

Perhaps the delegates thought Mr. Cousins did not have his heart in it. The arguments against were totally unconvincing and deference to the platform had only some of its usual effect. The sponsors refused to withdraw the motion. On being put to the vote it was declared carried by 4,209,000 to 3,683,000. The 40-hour week, as an *immediate* objective, was again the official policy of the Congress.

The 1957 Congress carried without opposition a resolution in favour of a 40-hour week, and at the 1958 Congress a motion urging that a special conference should be called with the aim of arriving at a unified policy for the promotion of the 40-hour week was remitted to the General Council. The following year the General Council reported that when they had considered this motion they had reiterated their belief that the way in which the 40-hour week was to be achieved was primarily a matter for individual unions. They took the view that a "TUC campaign might well be an embarrassment to unions, which needed to maintain flexibility in negotiating on a wide range of issues". There was no hint in the General Council's report that only a few years earlier the TUC had been urging that there should be legislation for a 40-hour week. The emphasis now was on the approaches being made by individual unions. There was no suggestion that the General Council might be in breach of the TUC's constitution. There was certainly no self-criticism of a job poorly and ineffectively done.

At the 1959 Congress a new note of urgency on the 40-hour week was sounded—once again. It came from Mr. George Lowthian, of the Amalgamated Union of Building Trade Workers and himself a member of the General Council. He moved a successful motion on behalf of his union deploring the continued resistance of employers to the introduction of a shorter working week. A maximum 40-hour week without loss of pay was, said the motion, not only economically possible but was an urgent necessity. The motion requested the General Council to inform the Government, industrialists and all concerned of the grave concern of the unions about the need for a shorter working week and of their intention to achieve it.

Mr. Lowthian was forthright in moving the motion. The motion indicated, he said, a change of emphasis. The TUC itself should move from "a negative to a positive attitude". It would be irresponsible in face of the concerted opposition of the employers, for each union to present its case as circumstances permitted. The Congress, said Mr. Lowthian, should sound a call to action.

Other speakers in the discussion took up the same theme. Indeed, an amendment was moved, though subsequently defeated, urging that the General Council should arrange for the transfer of staff from the TUC Production Department to the Organisation Department for the purpose of organising a campaign for the 40-hour week.

The 1959 Congress was also reminded by Mr. Bryn Roberts, the general secretary of the National Union Public Employees, of the earlier policy of Congress in favour of the achievement of a 40-hour week by a combination of legislative and voluntary action. He recalled that in 1947 the campaign was suspended but it had never been intended that it should be ended. It was cocooned for 12 years and in danger of becoming a stable chrysalis. Mr.

Roberts moved a motion urging that the claim for the 40-hour week should be pursued by Congress itself and not left to be dealt with by the separate affiliated unions.

The General Council supported Mr. Lowthian's motion but opposed Mr. Roberts' amendment. A number of unions, they pointed out, were already involved in important negotiations or claims for a shorter working week. The spokesman of the General Council in replying to the debate did not refer to Mr. Roberts' reminder of the earlier agitation for legislation—which was prudent in the light of the delays and changes of policy.

In November 1959 the General Council issued a reasoned statement in favour of the 40-hour week. It recalled that at the end of the Second World War "the General Council decided that the establishment of the 40-hour week should be pursued principally by way of direct claims by unions to employers, followed at the appropriate time by an approach to the Government with a request for legislation".

The General Council's statement referred to the movement towards a shorter working week in many other countries and pointed out that discussion on the reduction of working hours had been re-opened at the ILO. Until recently, said the General Council, Britain had not shared in the movement towards a shorter working week. The statement then went on to argue the case for reduced hours of work and referred to the rise in productivity.

In 1960 the movement towards a shorter working week gained considerable momentum. In the first 3 months of 1960 settlements for a reduction in the working week of about five million workers were reported. The general trend was to reduce basic working hours from about 44 to about 42 per week without loss of pay.

With the partial success of the shorter working week movement interest began to quicken in the demand for longer holidays. In 1960 the TUC carried a motion moved by the Watermen, Lightermen, Tugmen and Bargemen's Union supporting the principle of a third week's holiday throughout industry. The General Council supported the motion, though with a speech from Mr. Harry

Douglass (now Lord Douglass) emphasising that many unions would regard the winning of a shorter working week as of greater priority.

At the 1961 TUC a motion calling upon the General Council to institute a vigorous campaign for the 40-hour week—this time moved by the National Union of Mineworkers—was carried without opposition. Another resolution was also carried encouraging affiliated unions to press for a minimum 3 weeks' annual holiday and 8 statutory holidays for their members. The resolution, which was moved by the Amalgamated Engineering Union, noted that Britain had fallen "behind many other industrial countries in the matter of paid holidays".

The mover of the AEU motion, Mr. W. Cockin, recalled that even so far back in history as 1552 "some 27 days were appointed by law during which all kinds of labour ceased". There was certainly food for thought, he said, in the reflection that medieval society could afford holidays that modern society with all its vaunted technical and economic achievements seemed unable to afford. Mr. Cockin went on to compare the number of days holiday received by British workers with the number received by workers in Europe. In Britain, he said, manual workers generally received 18 days' holiday annually or 16 days if they were employed on a 5-day week. In France, it was 25–31 days; in West Germany, 25–28 days; in Italy, 31 days; in Sweden, 29 days; in Belgium, 22 days; in Finland, 28–30 days; in Denmark, 26–27 days; in Holland and Norway, 28 days.

In November 1961 the General Council of the TUC issued a circular to all affiliated unions providing information to assist unions intending to give high priority to the claim for a third week's holiday. The circular referred to the fact that, taking paid holidays into account, British manual workers had a lower total of paid holidays than workers in most countries in western Europe. Eleven important countries, they pointed out, including the USA, had longer holidays than Britain. The figures quoted by the TUC differed slightly from those quoted by Mr. Cockin at the 1961 Congress but the conclusion was the same. Sweden and

Norway, said the TUC circular, already enjoyed 29 days total paid holiday compared with Britain's 18 days for most workers. Moreover, as the TUC pointed out, a commission in Sweden was considering the introduction of a fourth week's holiday.

The General Council also drew attention in their circular to the practice in a number of other countries of giving extra holidays to young people and to workers in arduous or hazardous occupations. For example, in Germany and Austria workers of under 18 years of age received an extra 12 days. In France and Belgium, young workers received 6 extra days. In Norway, Sweden and Belgium underground workers also had additional days. But the General Council's *ex-cathedra* statements once again seemed merely to be endorsing what was being done. They were late, too late.

Meanwhile in the ILO the British workers' representatives had been playing a leading part in pressing for new international standards for a shorter working week. In 1961 a draft Recommendation was prepared laying down the 40-hour week as a social standard to be reached, without reduction in pay, and recommending the progressive reduction of hours, particularly where heavy physical or mental strain or health risks were involved. Unfortunately, when the text of the Recommendation was put to the ILO conference on its final day so many of the delegates had left that there was no quorum.

The draft Recommendation was, however, examined again during the ILO conference in the following year. A number of amendments were made to it, but in the view of the workers' delegations they did not weaken the intention of the draft. This time when put to the full conference the Recommendation was adopted by 255 votes to 22, with 46 abstentions including the two delegates representing the United Kingdom Government.

Subsequently in a White Paper (Command 1993), the British Government stated that it did not accept the Reduction of Hours of Work Recommendation. The preamble of this Recommendation, it pointed out, referred to the 40-hour week as a social standard to be reached by stages if necessary. The operative part of the Recommendation was in two sections. The first dealt with general principles. It provided that normal hours of work should be progressively reduced, when appropriate, with the ultimate aim of attaining the social standard indicated in the preamble without any reduction in wages. Member states, the Recommendation said, should formulate and pursue a national policy designed to promote by appropriate methods the adoption of the principle of the progressive reduction of the normal hours of work; they should also promote and, in so far as was consistent with national conditions and practice, ensure the application of this principle. The second section of the Recommendation dealt with methods of application.

The Government's reason for not accepting the Recommendation was put forward in the following terms:

> The provision of the Recommendation which requires Governments to formulate and pursue a national policy designed to promote the progressive reduction of hours of work is not consistent with the methods by which conditions of employment are normally determined in the United Kingdom.

Trade unionists who argue that the claim for a shorter working week is one which ought to be pursued exclusively through the machinery of collective bargaining and that government intervention ought not to be sought can thus find complete support for their view in the attitude of the then British Conservative Government in rejecting an international standard which was accepted at the ILO by an overwhelming majority. They knew on which side their employers' bread was buttered.

The reason advanced by the British Government for rejecting the Reduction of Hours of Work Recommendation was not only reactionary (in the full sense of that oft misused term) but it also did less than justice to the tradition, to which men of all parties in Britain have contributed, that the State *has* a responsibility to promote improved conditions of employment and light the beacons for others. There is not one but many Acts of Parliament bearing testimony to the past strength of this tradition. For the State to promote and pioneer improved conditions of employment is not to imply that it should usurp every function of the collective bargaining process. It is, however, to recognise that legislative and voluntary action both have a part to play in improving social conditions.

At the 1962 Congress a motion calling for a national campaign for a 40-hour week, under the co-ordination of the General Council, and for the achievement of a 35-hour week in the not too distant future was remitted, now ritualistically, to the General Council. After the motion had been moved and seconded the president asked the Congress delegates to agree to its remission to the General Council. "We think it would be an imposition", said the president, "on a union's programme of business if we sought to intervene in this way. Nor should we, as we see it, be able to mount the kind of national campaign for which he (the mover of the motion) asks."

The following year, at the 1963 Congress, the TUC adopted a composite resolution dealing both with reduced hours of work and with longer holidays. The resolution endorsed the statement of the General Council that the National Incomes Commission—which had been established by the Government in 1962—had neither the competence nor the authority to investigate agreements which had been reached by the process of collective bargaining. But the very existence of this shortlived Commission helped to push the motion through: it was a snub to the Government.

The National Incomes Commission reference arose from the decision of the Government in December 1962 to request the Commission to examine agreements for a reduction in normal working hours negotiated by the Scottish section of the National Federation of Building Trades Operatives and the Plumbing Trades Union. The unions concerned sought the advice of the TUC on an invitation which they had received to appear before the Commission. It was then that the General Council stated that in their view "the Commission had neither the competence nor the authority to investigate agreements which had been reached by processes of collective bargaining". This view was communicated to all affiliated unions.

At the 1964 Congress the General Council was able to report that there had been a quickening of the trend towards the 40-hour week for manual workers. A feature of the recent period, they pointed out, was the growth in the number of "long-term" agreements covering periods of 2 years or more and which provided for progressive reductions in hours and increases in holidays. The General Council estimated that about 1 million manual workers were employed in industries operating a 40-hour week or were covered by agreements for its introduction. In addition, many non-manual workers were employed for a basic working week of less than 40 hours.

The General Council pointed out in a further section of their report that about 96 per cent of manual workers in Britain covered by collective agreements or Wages Regulation Orders were entitled to a basic holiday with pay for 2 weeks. Of these about 15 per cent were in industries in which there was provision for additional days of holiday, dependent on the length of the worker's service with the same employer. A small number of industries, it was reported, had agreed to the gradual introduction of a third week's holiday by means of an additional day (or days) each year. It was noted that in the industries covered by Wages Councils much less progress than elsewhere had been made towards a 40-hour week and 3 weeks' holiday. This delay was a direct product of poor union organisation.

In 1964 Congress adopted a resolution calling upon the General Council to give all possible assistance to the efforts of affiliated unions to reduce the working year by achieving a progressive reduction of working hours to 35 a week without loss of pay and longer annual holidays of not less than 3 weeks' duration. The motion was moved by Mr. J. L. Jones of the Transport and General Workers' Union. He said that progress had been very slow, particularly on holidays, and that the unions had shown "amazing moderation". Mr. Jones was right, over and over again.

In their report to the 1965 Congress the General Council stated that in the previous 12 months "marked progress had been made towards the achievement of the 40-hour week and the 3 weeks' holiday". The Ministry of Labour, it was said, now estimated that about 25 per cent of manual workers had more than 2 weeks' basic annual holiday. Of workers who were entitled to a basic holiday of 2 weeks it was estimated that 22 per cent were in industries in which there was provision for additional days of holiday depending on the length of the individual worker's service with the same employer. The proportion of manual workers covered by collective agreements or statutory orders for a 40-hour week was about 33 per cent.

The 1965 Congress carried a resolution, moved by the National Union of Sheet Metal Workers and Coppersmiths and seconded by the Amalgamated Society of Boilermakers, Shipwrights, Blacksmiths and Structural Workers, which said that the "need to include the reduction of working hours and increased holidays within the framework of a planned economy is essential to the maintenance of the right of workers to more leisure time". The resolution requested the General Council to assist affiliated unions by ensuring that reduced working hours and longer holidays were included as essential features of a balanced socialist plan for industry.

The Shipping Dispute

Before the next Congress was to meet Britain was to have one of its most prolonged and significant stoppages of work for many years in a national dispute. The National Union of Seamen withdrew the labour of their members—as they returned to port—commencing from 16 May 1966. The strike lasted until midnight on 1 July. One of the central issues in the dispute was the claim of the union for the introduction of a 40-hour week.

There were two special features of this dispute worthy of note in the light of the frequently reaffirmed support of the trade union and labour movement for the 40-hour week. The first was the hostility of the Labour Government towards the seamen's claim.

The Prime Minister sought to incite prejudice by diverting attention from the real issues of the dispute and attacking what he described as a "tightly knit group of politically motivated men" who were responsible for prolonging the stoppage. A few individuals, he said, had brought pressure to bear on a select few on the Executive Council of the National Union of Seamen, who in turn "have been able to dominate the majority of that otherwise sturdy union". Needless to say, the National Union of Seamen rejected this allegation with the contempt it deserved. They pointed out, time and time again, that they were engaged in an industrial dispute in support of their claim for a 40-hour week.

The second feature of the dispute was the very evident reluctance of the TUC to support the NUS in the firm stand they took for the 40-hour week. The claim for the 40-hour week was not only the traditional policy of the Congress but—as already pointed out earlier in this chapter—it is also included as an object of the Congress in the rules and standing orders. Rule 2 states that the Congress shall endeavour to establish "a legal maximum working week of 40 hours".

The report of the General Council to the 1966 Congress indicated the extent of the General Council's unwillingness to support the firm demands of the NUS. The executive of the NUS, it was reported, had rejected the first report of the Court of Inquiry and had stated "that there would be no return to work unless the 40-hour week was granted now and the Sundays at sea leave agreement remained intact". In lengthy discussions between the union's Executive Committee and the Finance and General Purposes Committee the General Secretary of the TUC

> stated that without some movement on the part of the union it was impossible for the General Council to assist. He explained to the representatives that it was not for an affiliated union to lay down its terms and then claim the unqualified support of the TUC. The General Council's support would be given to those things which the General Council could support and those things must have a practical element. The NUS seemed to be calling upon the General Council for unqualified support and this could not be given to any union.

The seamen's point of view was put to the 1966 Congress by their general secretary, Mr. W. Hogarth, and by one of their leading sea-going members, Mr. J. Kenny. Mr. Hogarth expressed his appreciation of the efforts of the TUC, and of Mr. Woodcock in particular, to find a solution to the dispute. Of the Government's attitude Mr. Hogarth said:

... our strike was a strike against our members' employers and not the Government. It was not a strike against the Government or the nation at all. It was the Prime Minister himself in his broadcast of May 16th—the first day of our strike, by the way—who dubbed it as a strike against the State.

The Government treated this dispute as if it was a direct challenge to their incomes policy, instead of an attempt by members of the National Union of Seamen to win a 40-hour week for themselves at sea. The introduction of the charge by Mr. Wilson that some of my executive councillors were influenced by a "tightly-knit group of politically motivated men" was, to say the least, ill-timed, and the only effect on the NUS was to harden our members' attitude to the dispute and so prolong the strike. Perhaps one of the greatest tragedies of the dispute was the inability of the Ministry of Labour to carry out its traditional and vital conciliatory function. The Minister and his civil service colleagues did their utmost, but in my opinion were all the time severely handicapped by the Cabinet's determination to prevent our members from gaining their demands. I think that this taking away of the Ministry of Labour's role in industrial disputes is upsetting all the balance and can have a serious effect in the sphere of industrial relations.

Mr. Kenny replied to the statement of the General Council that it was "not for an affiliated union to lay down its terms and then claim the unqualified support of the TUC". He said:

The General Council—and I do not mean to be critical of the General Council, but I just want to say this—tell us that it was not for an affiliated union to lay down its terms and then claim the unqualified support of the TUC. This suggests to me that the National Union of Seamen was obviously asking for something rather outrageous and extravagant. In fact, the basic demand of the seamen was for a 40-hour week, a demand which many of you people sitting here have already obtained or will in the very near future. Yet the most the employers were prepared to do was to grant the 40-hour week in 1968, provided the seamen were prepared to give up 17 days' paid leave in order to obtain it. In all your experience you know that the 40-hour week has been granted without any loss of wages or earnings. So you can see that we, as seamen, were in a very invidious position indeed.

I ask you this question: were we wrong in trying to get the 40-hour week, when many unions had already obtained it? Were we wrong in objecting to the retrograde step of obtaining it in two years' time by

giving up our paid leave? We must have been wrong. I resent the implica-
tion of the General Council's report to this Congress that the seamen
were demanding impossible conditions and that until they were prepared
to whittle down their demands nothing could be done to help them.

The General Council of the TUC reported to the 1966 Congress that about 50 per cent of manual workers covered by collective agreements or statutory orders would be on a basic 40-hour
week by the end of 1966. In addition, said the General Council, "it
is known that many non-manual workers have a normal week of
35 to 38 hours". The General Council also reported that about
30 per cent of manual workers now had more than 2 weeks' basic
annual holiday with pay. In addition, about one-third of the
workers entitled to only 2 weeks' annual holiday were in industries where they were entitled to additional days of holiday
depending on the length of the individual worker's service with the
same employer.

Hours of Work Since the War

The reduction in the length of the basic working week since the
end of the Second World War has taken place in three main
phases. Between 1946 and 1950 hours were reduced in many
industries from 47 or 48 to 44 or 45. Between 1960 and 1962 there
was a further reduction, generally to 42 or 42½ hours per week. The
latest phase, for the reduction to 40 hours, can, perhaps, be said to
have begun from 1962. In the autumn of that year the 40-hour
week was introduced in the general printing industry. (This was
not, by any means, the first agreement for a 40-hour week, but it
was the first *major* agreement covering many different firms and
tens of thousands of workers.) In 1963 a number of agreements
were concluded for the introduction of the 40-hour week in two
stages. In 1964 the movement for reduced hours of work gathered
momentum and many more agreements were concluded. Britain's
largest single industry—engineering—introduced a 40-hour week
in the summer of 1965. By the beginning of 1967 about a half of
Britain's manual workers had won a basic 40-hour week. This,
however, is only another way of saying that there are still millions

of workers whose basic working week is longer than 40 hours. This does not reflect credit on Britain.

Despite the phased reduction in the length of the basic working week since the end of the Second World War there was only a slight reduction in average weekly hours worked until the Labour Government's deflationary policy began to take effect. Indeed, the average weekly hours worked for all workers in 1964, when Labour came to power, were about the same as in 1950. Actual hours worked rose slightly between 1950 and 1955 and then decreased slightly until the early part of 1963. After that they again rose. They have fallen consistently since October 1964. In October 1964 the average weekly hours worked by adult male manual workers covered by the Ministry of Labour inquiries were 47·7 per week. The latest returns—for October 1966—show that this figure had fallen to 46·0 hours per week. Separate returns for agriculture, which are not included in the above figures, show that the average weekly hours of hired regular whole-time agricultural workers in England and Wales for the year April 1965 to March 1966 were 50·3 for men of 20 years of age and over. The yearly average figures includes hours paid for but not actually worked, e.g. paid holidays.

From these figures it is clear that for a great many workers the reduction in the length of the basic working week has resulted not in more leisure but in higher earnings. This, it cannot be emphasised too strongly, is not and should not be the purpose of trade union claims for a shorter working week. Persistent overtime ultimately undermines the strength of trade union claims for adequate basic rates of pay: workers become conditioned to a pay packet which includes overtime earnings. In the long term, persistent overtime does not make for higher productivity: it may even relatively reduce it. Frequently it provides an excuse, or a safety hatch, for poor management planning. It gives an impression of industriousness, when in reality management has failed to achieve the necessary higher rate of productivity by improved methods and the elimination of inefficiency. Persistent overtime also makes for a higher accident rate and for absenteeism.

The British need, to use the good planner's maxim, is to work "smarter not longer".

Unions in a number of industries, notably engineering, have offered to enter into joint arrangements with employers for the control, limitation and reduction of overtime. All too often, however, employers have rejected any such proposals. They regard the control of overtime as the prerogative of management and this they guard with religious intensity.

The Case for Improvements

The case for a 40-hour week and a minimum 3 weeks' holiday rests, fundamentally, on the right of workers to share in the benefits of increased productivity made possible by technical progress and to take part of this share in the form of increased leisure to develop their personal culture. Indeed, our sights

TABLE 2

	Total output of goods and services 1958 = 100
1950	85·7
1951	87·6
1952	87·0
1953	90·5
1954	94·3
1955	97·5
1956	98·4
1957	100·1
1958	100·0
1959	104·5
1960	110·1
1961	112·1
1962	113·5
1963	117·3
1964	124·3
1965	127·7
1966	129·2

should now be adjusted to a lower hours figure. Even in Britain, where the rate of increase in production has not been outstanding, there has, nevertheless, been a significant increase in output over the years. Table 2, taken from the official *Statistics on Incomes, Prices, Employment and Production*, illustrates the trend.

Over a period of 15 years total output of goods and services has risen by about 50 per cent. During this same period the increase in the working population rose by just over 10 per cent. There has, therefore, been a significant rise in productivity per person employed. A table published in the March 1967 issue of *Statistics on Incomes, Prices, Employment and Production* shows that the gross domestic product per head of the labour force rose, at constant prices, by more than 38 per cent between 1950 and 1965. This represents a rate of increase of about $2 \cdot 2$ per cent per annum compound.

Long hours of work, we repeat, do not, in the long term, contribute to high productivity. A report on *Reduction of Hours of Work* prepared by the ILO in 1956 pointed out that experience during both world wars confirmed earlier experience that the working of excessively long hours defeats its own purpose. The ILO report said:

> During brief spurts it is possible to draw on the reserve strength of workers and to obtain greatly increased output. Over an extended period nature takes its revenge. It seems clear that, in general, when the working week is so long that it imposes great fatigue and strain on workers, a reduction in hours will lead in the long run to an increase in output, not merely per hour, but also per week, i.e. hourly output will increase sufficiently to offset the reduction in hours worked.

A report entitled *About Fitting the Job to the Worker* published by OEEC in 1961 made much the same point:

> For too long, people accepted the view that production was in direct proportion to the length of the working day. Whenever the work in hand could not be completed in the normal hours, the first step was invariably to resort to overtime.
> Obviously, viewed in this light, the solution of the problem is both simple and attractive. However, production does not increase in proportion to the number of hours worked. The mistake has unfortunate consequences for the workers' health and the firm's profits.

The problem is quite different when it is a matter of determining, for the various types of work, the daily output which an individual can achieve without damaging his health, even in the very long run, and without aging prematurely.

The information collected is revealing. In the first place, too much overtime causes overwork and premature aging in the operative. For the firm, overtime imposes a heavy financial burden, as it is not usually profitable. In addition, the highest percentage of accidents occurs when extra time is worked. Operatives working overtime have to take more sick leave than normal.

Modern production methods in industry have, for millions of workers, increased the fatigue of labour. Even where the intensity of manual effort has been reduced by modern machinery the new evils are often boredom and monotony. Craftsmanship has been eliminated except for a minority of workers. Most factory workers are today engaged in jobs which are repetitive and do nothing to stimulate their creative instincts. Workers ought not to be required, except in emergencies or special circumstances, to work more than 40 hours per week in such jobs. They are already becoming alienated from their work.

The growth of productivity in modern industry has not only made increased leisure possible; it has also made it essential if workers are to live a full, rounded and satisfying life. The ILO report on *Reductions in Hours of Work* said:

The same forces—those making for higher productivity—which have made increased leisure possible over the last century have also made it more necessary for all those many workers whose jobs cannot, by their intrinsic nature, provide a main focus of interest in their lives or opportunities for self-expression or all-round development.

Much, of course, remains to be done in the provision of facilities for the development of the leisure time pursuits of the population. This is a task for the nation: the need is to encourage and provide facilities for education, sport, music, drama and other recreational activities.

More leisure is also necessary if democracy is to strike ever deeper roots among the population. Democracy does not mean only that citizens have the right periodically to mark a ballot paper. It implies that people actively participate in shaping their own way of life. Millions of citizens should share in running and controlling the various political parties, trade unions, the co-operative movement, the social services, church organisations, youth clubs, cultural groups, voluntary bodies and the various organs of local government in a way which is superior to the present system. Democracy, in this sense, requires a population which is both able and willing to undertake voluntary obligations to maintain a healthy and vigorous public life. This will never be achieved unless millions of ordinary citizens—and not just a few dedicated individuals—have the necessary amount of required leisure time and a minimum of knowledge to enable them to participate constructively in the organisations which interest them.

One of the strongest arguments for the introduction of a maximum 40-hour week is that it would stimulate management to increase the efficiency of British industry. It is no accident that generally hours of work are longest where the standard of managerial efficiency is lowest. Conversely, the firms which have pioneered reduced hours of work are nearly always well known for their efficiency and for the adoption of modern and highly productive methods.

British management techniques are all too frequently of a low standard. The effect of increasing the cost of labour is to make investment in new equipment more attractive. One of the criticisms sometimes made by American trade union leaders against the trade union movement in Britain is that British trade unionists have been too modest in their demands, particularly on hours of work, and that this has contributed to the backwardness of British industry and to the slow progress made since the war. The ILO report on *Reduction in Hours of Work*, 1956, said:

Sometimes the prospect of a reduction in output and a rise in unit costs as a result of shorter hours may stimulate managements to introduce improvements which would have been worth introducing before, but which were not previously introduced for various reasons. Already existing but unrealised opportunities for increasing productivity are no doubt substantial in all countries, especially among less enterprising firms, and wherever this is so, it is very possible that a determined effort to raise productivity may more than offset any unfavourable effects of shorter hours on output and costs. A rise in wages or in taxes, or anything else which threatens the financial stability of a business and administers a shock and a spur to management, may have an effect similar to that of a reduction in hours in stimulating greater efficiency.

One of the arguments which used to be heard more frequently against the claim for reduced hours of work is that British labour standards are already so far ahead of those of her continental trading rivals that any further improvement would result in British exports being priced out of the market. *The simple answer to this argument is that whatever may have been the position in earlier years it simply is not true today.* When account is taken of the length of the basic working week, of the average amount of overtime worked, and of the length of holidays, British industrial manual workers do not enjoy more leisure than the industrial manual workers of the main industrial countries of the Continent. If anything, the reverse is now the case and the process continues.

Nor is it true that wage costs per working hour in Britain are so high in comparison with other countries that no further improvements can be conceded to British workers without seriously jeopardising British exports. A table published in *The Times* of 18 April 1967 showed that in 1965 average wage costs per working hour in Britain, including both direct wage costs and additional indirect wage costs, were lower than in Sweden, West Germany, Norway, Denmark, the Netherlands, Italy, France and Belgium. Only in Austria, of the quoted European industrialised countries, were wage costs per working hour slightly lower than in Britain. Significantly in a number of industries, including foodstuffs, beverages, paper, chemicals, building materials, shipyards and mining United Kingdom wage costs were the lowest of any quoted country.

However, the same unfavourable comparison—particularly for hours of work—cannot be made for the majority of salaried workers in Britain. This is mainly for historical reasons but it is also related to the specific militancy of certain non-manual unions. Hours of work for many salaried workers in Britain—probably the majority—are less than on the Continent. They are also less in many cases than in the United States. In the engineering industry in Britain, for example, the maximum basic working week for hundreds of thousands of salaried workers (but not always including works staff) has been $37\frac{1}{2}$ hours since the end of March 1965. In local government the basic working week for salaried staff is 38 hours and in the civil service it varies from $36\frac{1}{2}$ to 38 hours. In the civil service it is customary to refer to a working week of $41\frac{1}{2}$ to 43 hours, but this includes the midday meal break.

Holidays for salaried staff in British industry, on the other hand, compare unfavourably with the Continent. Industrial staff in Britain do not usually enjoy the same length of holidays as salaried staff in the public services, particularly the civil service.

With the development of productivity in industry, and with it an accelerated rate of technical progress, the introduction of a maximum 40-hour week in industry and commerce would provide a safeguard against unemployment. It would be a social catastrophe if the development of productivity led to more output, but with unnecessarily long hours of labour for the majority and unemployment for the minority. Those who are very optimistic that mass unemployment is a thing of the past should reflect on the fact that even within recent years unemployment has risen on a number of occasions to well over half a million. In each of the years 1958, 1959, 1962 and 1963 the annual average unemployment figure was more than 450,000 or 2 per cent of the labour force, reaching the highest annual post-war average of 573,200 in 1963. In the early part of 1967 unemployment exceeded 600,000.

The Example of the USA

In the United States, where technical progress has proceeded farthest, the relevance of reduced hours of work for the reduction of unemployment is even more obvious. The greater part of British industry, like the greater part of American industry, is privately owned with a high concentration of personal wealth and power and is conducted primarily for private profit; the experience of the United States is not, therefore, without lessons for Britain, despite the greater readiness of almost all sections of the community in Britain to accept the need for some form of economic planning.

In April 1964 *The American Federationist*, the official monthly magazine of the American Federation of Labour and Congress of Industrial Organisations, carried a lengthy report of American labour's campaign for a reduction of working hours. The aim of the campaign, it said, was clear, simple and direct—to spread job opportunities and reduce unemployment.

Unemployment in the USA, the AFL–CIO pointed out, had risen steadily in recent years and had doubled since 1953. Their estimate of total unemployment was as follows:

> In 1963 there were 4·2 million unemployed or 5·7 per cent of the civilian labour force. There were also 2·3 million additional workers who were compelled to work part-time because full-time work was not available to them. In addition, about 1 million to over 2 million men and women were neither employed nor counted as unemployed since they had given up seeking work because of the lack of job opportunities.
>
> When the figures are added up, it is estimated that about 8 per cent or more of available work-time in 1963 was lost as a result of insufficient job opportunities and part-time work.

On 11 June 1965 Mr. I. W. Abel, the new president of the United Steelworkers of America, commenting on the labour negotiations in the basic steel industry stated:

> The first and foremost thing is this: our workers are eagerly looking for a measure of security. There is great concern, this fear of automation, of technical change. In just this last 5 years we have had installations of machinery which would have been unbelievable a few years ago. For example a first helper or melter in the open hearth was set for life. It was seen as a highly skilled job. And then along comes this oxygen furnace and the jobs are gone.   Our highest priority is on retraining and some means of security.

The AFL–CIO calculated that between 1953 and 1963, despite increased production, nearly 4 million jobs disappeared in factory, mining and farm production and on the railways. The growth of employment in the various service occupations, such as distribution and commerce, failed to keep pace with the growth in the number of job seekers, including those displaced from "productive" industry and the new entrants to the labour market.

The AFL–CIO noted that the pace by which productivity was increasing in productive industry was being stepped up. Thanks to automation there were now machines that could remember, apply logic and arrive at conclusions. There were machines that inspected the products they were turning out, rejected them if they did not meet the required standards and corrected their own errors. There were even machines that changed their own parts when they broke down or wore out. And yet true automation was still in its infancy. There was every reason to believe that far more sweeping changes were ahead.

Rising productivity, said the AFL–CIO, could be either an enormous blessing or a source of great trouble and hardship. It could mean a higher standard of living and more leisure for all or, if there was a failure to adopt the proper policies, it could mean widespread labour displacement and rising unemployment. In the last decade the spread of automation in the USA had been accompanied by labour displacement and rising unemployment: since 1957 the unemployment figure has always been over 5 per cent in each year.

The AFL–CIO urged that priority should be given to the need for more jobs. An essential part of this effort was to reduce working hours. It was estimated that half a million jobs would be created in the USA for each 1-hour general reduction in the working week. This reduction in hours, it was stressed, should not lead to a reduction in pay, otherwise the fall in consumers' purchasing power would contribute to further unemployment.

Overall employment in the US has grown since the "Federationist" article, due mainly to the heating of the economy caused by the Vietnam war. With a political solution of that conflict the situation could be catastrophic for certain US industries.

The American unions are pressing strongly for a basic working week of less than 40 hours. About 15 per cent of American workers have already achieved this objective. The AFL–CIO estimated that in New York 20 per cent of the factory production labour force and 90 per cent of the office and clerical workers were on full-time schedules shorter than 40 hours. In Boston, the percentages were 12 for production workers and 65 for office workers; for Chicago, 6 and 41; for Philadelphia, 12 and 55; and for San Francisco 16 and 37. But for manual workers the pre-war 40-hour week remains the standard excepting the notable agreements for 36 hours in the Akron rubber plants, the lithographers' 35-hour week and the 25 hours worked by contracting electricians in New York City. The legal overtime rate is time and one-half, although the AFL–CIO is asking for double time after 40 hours while President Johnson offered this after 48 hours at first and after 45 hours later on. The US Department of Labour estimated that 42·5 million hours of overtime was worked by non-supervisory employees *weekly* in March 1964. This represented an average of 2·8 weekly overtime hours a head for production workers in manufacturing industry. By March 1965 it had climbed to 3·5 hours of overtime a week.

The Need in Britain

The need in Britain is for the introduction of a basic working week of not more than 40 hours, with *tight* controls on overtime working, and an annual holiday, excluding public holidays, of not less than 3 weeks with a perspective of a 35-hour week. Progress towards this objective should be by a combination of legislative and voluntary action, broadly on the lines advocated, in relation to the 40-hour week, in the 1944 report of the General Council of the TUC.

Legislation on the 40-hour week and 3 weeks' holiday should place on the Minister of Labour an obligation to secure a maximum 40-hour basic working week and a minimum 3 weeks' annual holiday, plus public holidays, for all employed persons within, say, 2 years of the passing of the Act. The legislation should empower the Minister:

(a) to recognise voluntary collective agreements for a 40-hour week or less and three weeks' holiday or more and to require all employers in the industry or trade concerned to

observe terms and conditions not less favourable than those
provided in the agreement;

(b) to require other industries, where no such agreement
existed, to submit a draft scheme, after consultations between employers and workers' organisations, for a basic
40-hour week and three weeks' holiday;

(c) to establish a Commission—perhaps the Industrial Court—
to advise on whether or not particular arrangements in an
industry or section of industry met the requirements of the
Act, and if not, to advise on what steps should be taken to
ensure that the intention of the Act was observed.

Legislation of this kind would not, except in cases where it was
needed, result in State interference in the normal process of collective bargaining. Moreover, it would enable industry itself to
work out its own arrangements to ensure that particular firms did
not evade the intention of the Act by systematic overtime at normal
rates of pay. Always the power of the Commission would be held
in reserve to be used only when the circumstances required it. In
reviewing the history of the post-war drive for shorter hours and
more holidays the sluggishness of the forward current and its lack
of direction are striking.

A Minimum Wage

In the rules and standing orders of the TUC one of the objects
of the Congress is defined as "a legal minimum wage for each
industry or occupation". Towards the end of 1966 a campaign for
a £15 national minimum wage was launched by the Transport and
General Workers' Union. In a speech at Central Hall, West-
minster, to branch representatives, Mr. Frank Cousins, the
General Secretary of the TGWU, explained the significance of
what he described as a "new drive for social justice". He said that
both sides of industry had set their sights too low and had not
produced either the prosperity or the efficiency of which Britain
was capable. The creation of a new central employers' body, the
Confederation of British Industry, had made it practical to talk

about central negotiations with the TUC on basic minimum wages, normal hours of employment, holidays and sick pay. The TGWU, said Mr. Cousins, would not dodge the responsibility of saying what was meant by a minimum wage. It must be at least £15 a week exclusive of overtime, shift payments, productivity bonuses and piece work. This figure, he said, was reasonable and urgent and must be established.

To those who said that British industry could not afford it Mr. Cousins' answer was: "Then British industry should be ashamed of itself. We have to make sure British industry can afford it, we have to get down to the necessary reorganisation."

In their campaign for a minimum wage of £15 the TGWU have argued that there is no room for complacency about the defects of the British system of industrial relations. A statement in the TGWU official magazine said: "The idea that high wages are a crime must be replaced with the recognition that they are a sign of progress and that low wages are a disgrace in themselves and usually evidence of old fashioned methods."

The TGWU pointed out when they launched their campaign that more than one-quarter of adult male workers earned less than £15 a week in total, and that the vast majority of wage agreements for basic minimum rates provided for much less. There are very few national wage agreements providing for £15 a week or more basic pay for men, and almost none for women. Some 6 million out of the 15 million men at work, according to the TGWU, earned less than £15 for a standard working week. The figures for 1965 have been analysed in detail by the TGWU and they show that in that year 30 per cent of adult male manual workers earned less than £15 per week including overtime payments. Other figures show that less than 8 per cent of women manual workers, aged 18 and over, earn more than £13 a week including overtime payments, and that 42·5 per cent of heads of households had incomes of less than £15. More than one-quarter of all families had less than £15 a week.

In July 1967 the publication by the Ministry of Social Security of the report of an Inquiry into the *Circumstances of Families* confirmed the widespread existence of poverty. This report revealed that in the summer of 1966 there were probably half a million families, containing up to 1¼ million children, whose incomes, excluding National Assistance, was less than would be paid to a family in the summer of 1967 which qualified for supplementary benefit. Half a million children were in families whose fathers were in full-time work or who were unemployed or sick but who were disqualified from receiving their requirements measured by supplementary benefit standards because of the "wage stop". In other words their wages when working were at a very low level.

Since the launching of the £15 national minimum wage campaign there has been considerable discussion in trade union and other circles on the implications of a national minimum wage. In an article in *The Times* on 28 March 1967, Professor Hugh Clegg, a member of the National Board for Prices and Incomes, pointed out that there are pockets of low-paid workers in most industries. They were not to be found exclusively in the industries where wages councils had been established. Professor Clegg referred to an article published by Mr. Derek Robinson in the February issue of the *Bulletin of the Oxford University Institute of Economics and Statistics*. Mr. Robinson's figures suggested that nearly all industries pay some of their male workers less than £11 a week and many have large numbers earning less than £15.

Professor Clegg pointed out that what could be done for lower paid workers depended to some extent upon the consequences of an increase for them upon the pay of other workers. He said that if it were possible to raise the earnings of all adult male workers below £15 to that figure without increasing the pay of anyone else the cost, according to Mr. Robinson's figures, would be equivalent to an increase of 1·36 per cent in the average earnings of adult males. On the other hand, a national minimum of £15 would provide an increase of £5 per week for men earning at present only £10. If all differentials were to be maintained the total increase in the wage bill might be as high as one-third. The extent to which there would be consequential increases would depend upon how far differentials were maintained. Some differentials, based on skill and responsibility, would have to be maintained. Others, based on company or plant rates, would not be affected to anything like the same extent. Professor Clegg's conclusion was that the consequence of a £15 minimum would be a surge in wage costs and prices which would benefit no one, not even the lowest paid, but that a minimum of £10 10s. 0d. or £11 would probably be manageable. Over a period of time this national minimum could be increased.

The effect on women's wages would be so great that, in Professor Clegg's view, there would have to be one minimum for men and another for women. Equal pay, he said, was a subject for hypocrisy, no less in countries where men pretend that they want it than in countries where they pretend to have it. Nevertheless, if Britain really wanted to move towards equal pay a national minimum wage would provide an effective instrument for achieving it. The national minimum for women could be moved by stages towards the national minimum for men.

A National Minimum and "Equal Pay"

The introduction of a realistic national minimum wage would be an extremely important step towards improving the very low average wage received by women workers in industry. It would thus be a significant advance towards equal pay for equal work. Both the Labour Party and the TUC are committed to the principle of equal pay for equal work. During the course of the 1964 General Election the Labour Party issued a leaflet entitled *The Charter of Rights*. It declared: "Labour will bring in a new Charter of Rights for all employed in industry, commerce and public service, giving: [*as the last of seven 'rights': C. J., J. E. M.]* The right to equal pay for equal work." At the 1963 Party Conference the National Executive Committee accepted a motion asking for a legislative initiative to provide equal pay throughout industry and commerce within a specified period. It also demanded that the ILO Convention covering the issue, namely

Convention 100, should be ratified. The 1963 TUC also accepted a resolution which called upon the next Labour Government to ratify ILO Convention 100 on "equal pay for work of equal value" by a legislative initiative within a specified period.

In November 1964, shortly after the election of the Labour Government, the General Council of the TUC wrote to the Minister of Labour drawing his attention to Congress policy and inquiring how the Government proposed to implement the ILO Convention and to give effect to the Labour Party's election promise that equal pay would be part of a Charter of Rights for all employees.

The attitude of the Government throughout has been to affirm that they support the principle of equal pay for work of equal value, but to maintain that its introduction is a task of great magnitude involving complex economic and social issues. In particular, the Government have said that the problem should be examined in relation to the economic situation of the country and the prices and incomes policy. They have also said that it has not been possible to secure agreement from the principal employers' organisations and the TUC as to what is meant by equal pay for equal work.

The Government have had discussions with the TUC on the introduction of equal pay for equal work and have said that the general objective can only be gradually achieved. The Minister of Labour maintained that it was not the policy of the Government to ratify the ILO Convention until the conditions existed for it to have some practical meaning. If, however, agreement could be reached on a broad plan of action the Government might then consider ratification.

The TUC and the Confederation of British Industry agreed to participate in tripartite discussions with the Ministry to examine certain of the technical problems associated with the introduction of equal pay. In reply to a parliamentary question on 10 July 1967, the Minister of Labour confirmed that he had received the report of this joint working party. He again supported the principle of the rate for the job, but pointed to difficulties in its application. He said that it had to be related to the prices and incomes policy of the Government in the present economic situation, and he added that both sides of industry had failed to tell the Government what they both meant by equal pay.

More than 3 years after the election of a Labour Government pledged to the introduction of equal pay nothing effective has been done to implement it. The Government have resorted to the evasions and shufflings of earlier administrations. It is self-evident that women's elementary plea for justice will not be answered except as a result of constant pressure from all sections of the trade union and labour movement. At the 1966 TUC a resolution was again carried calling for the implementation of the principle of equal pay. It said that it had now become urgently necessary. The mover of the motion, Mrs. L. Teague, speaking for the National Union of Tailors and Garment Workers, pointed out that by 1 January 1966 no fewer than fifty-one member States of the ILO had ratified Convention 100. These fifty-one states did not include the United Kingdom.

Criticisms

The case for a national minimum wage has not received universal support in trade union circles. In the April 1967 issue of the *AEU Journal*, for example, there was an article with the title "Is the Minimum Wage a Practical Proposition Today?" It was prepared by the AEU Research Department. The article acknowledged that there was a substantial number of people in Britain living below the National Assistance standard. The number might be as high as 7 or 8 million people. The *AEU Journal* article then discussed ways whereby these poverty-stricken families could be helped. It pointed out that the establishment of a national minimum wage would still leave out of account families where there was not a wage-earner. The article said: "and would there not be the very real danger that these unfortunates would tend to be forgotten if the trade unions centred their efforts on raising wages as an answer to poverty? This has certainly been the experience of the past."

The article went on to argue that to raise earnings to a basic minimum of £15 a week would lead to a substantial increase in costs in manufacturing industry. Prices would probably rise by some hundreds of millions of pounds. To raise the average to £14 for the 8 million or so women in employment would mean an increase of around £1,500,000,000 per annum in wage costs. Any substantial increase in costs, said the article, would have a drastic effect on Britain's balance of trade.

The AEU article emphasised that many differentials would have to be maintained because they serve a real economic purpose. They include differentials based upon differences of skill. The article said that the present wage structure with its inbuilt differentials should not be regarded as inviolate, but nevertheless any radical changes could only be achieved over a considerable period of time. The article added: "It would indeed make sense to base a national plan on the assumption that minimum wages and social security payments should rise faster than average earnings, but we must recognise that this is a long term objective."

The conclusion of the article was that it was a desirable social aim to seek a redistribution of national income in favour of the poorer members of society, but that to propose a national minimum wage without changing the share of wages in the national income was to invite worsening conditions for better paid sections of the working class. This, the article said, "Does not provide a ready appeal to many trade unionists. It was the responsibility of the nation as a whole to provide a solution to the problem of poverty and much could be done at once to resolve this unnecessary social evil without adding significantly to public expenditure or wage costs." The article suggested that the present national insurance contribution from workers should be abolished because it acts as a sharply regressive tax. The burden is proportionately greater for those with the lowest wages. The tax, it was suggested, should be replaced by wage related contributions for social security benefits.

The article also urged that tax allowances for children should be reduced and higher family allowances introduced, with perhaps the value of family allowances inversely related to family income.

Need for a National Minimum

The arguments advanced by Professor Clegg and in the article in the *AEU Journal* have some force, but they do not, nevertheless, provide an adequate reason for resisting the demand for a national minimum wage considerably higher than the £10 10*s*. 0*d*. or £11 suggested by Professor Clegg. Ever since the dawn of the industrial system there have been arguments advanced by economists to justify low wages, but in modern Britain there can be no social justification for the existence of widespread poverty. Low wages, far from assisting British industry, serve only to accommodate poor management, low efficiency and out-of-date methods. The TGWU have performed a public service by launching their campaign for a £15 national minimum wage. Despite the undoubted difficulties and problems the strategic aim of this campaign is right. Far too many workers in Britain receive wages which are so low as to be a public disgrace.

CHAPTER 8

Laws we do not need—
the Prices and Incomes Acts

THE Labour Government elected in 1964 was not the first British government to attempt to hold down wages. Even during the period between the two world wars governments sought from time to time to stop wages rising or even to impose or encourage wage reductions. This occurred on a number of occasions in the 1920's and again in 1931. Always governments plead that they take such action in the national interest.

The efforts of successive governments to influence wage determination since the end of the Second World War have been more persistent. What has distinguished these efforts from those of earlier periods has been that they have been pursued more systematically, that they have been supported by arguments designed to appeal to trade unionists, and—since the election of the present Labour Government—they have been buttressed by legislation.

Arguments and Counter-arguments

The arguments for an incomes policy designed to restrain wages have been outlined in a number of official statements since 1945. The latest version was contained in the Joint Statement of Intent on Productivity, Prices and Incomes signed by the Government, the TUC and representatives of the principal employers' organisations in December 1964.

Briefly the argument advanced in this document was that Britain's economic situation was extremely unsatisfactory and that drastic measures were necessary to close the deficit in the balance of payments. Britain, it was said, must encourage exports and sharpen her competitive ability. Urgent and vigorous action would have to be taken to raise productivity throughout industry and commerce, to keep increases in total money income in line with real national output and to maintain a stable general price level. The Government said they would place greater emphasis on the need to increase productivity and would set up machinery to keep a continuous watch on the general movement of prices and of money incomes of all kinds. The employers' representatives and the TUC undertook, in turn, to co-operate with the Government in keeping under review the general movement of prices and money incomes and to help in giving effective shape to the machinery to be established by the Government for the examination of movements in prices and money incomes.

A reply to this Joint Statement of Intent was published by five white-collar technical unions, namely the Association of Cinematograph and Television Technicians, the Association of Scientific Workers, ASSET, DATA, and the Society of Technical Civil Servants. Their reply was published as a pamphlet under the title *A Declaration of Dissent*.* The substance of this reply is, in our view, still valid. It is worth recalling what the main points of the reply were.

First, the *Declaration of Dissent* challenged the contention that Britain now has a planned economy. Planning, it said, does not consist of controlling one element in a situation, with very little control over other equally essential elements and without much control over the environment. Britain was still predominantly an unplanned society. It was given direction by exhortation and bridle. Such guidance as was given by the Government and by the National Economic Development Council consisted largely, over the greater part of industry and commerce, of an indication of the probable pattern of development in the years ahead. The Government's influence on economic affairs was, nevertheless, often

* Followed by two other publications: *Counsel's Opinion on the Prices and Incomes Act* and *The Bad Package* (a criticism of the supporting economic and political policies).

swamped by the main consideration influencing economic decisions in the private firms who own at least 80 per cent of British industry and commerce. This main consideration remained the desire to maximise profits.

Events since the publication of the Joint Statement of Intent have shown how right were the warnings sounded in the *Declaration of Dissent* about the ineffectiveness of the Government's so-called economic planning. The national plan became out of date almost as soon as it was published. The decisions of the great majority of firms in British industry and commerce are not taken according to the directives of the Government but according to profit considerations. The one element in the situation on which there has been far more effective control has been wages. The suggestion of the Government that it is possible to persuade companies to increase their profits *only* as a result of increased efficiency is not borne out by experience. The *Declaration of Dissent* asked whether most private firms would be expected, or requested, or exhorted to make lower profits than they would if they followed their noimal business motives. This, it pointed out, they would have to do *deliberately* to satisfy the wording of the Joint Statement of Intent. This, however, is an utterly unrealistic basis for any kind of long or medium term policy. In the middle and long run, firms obey market forces.

The *Declaration of Dissent* pointed to the gross inequality which already disfigures British society. This inequality, it said, ought to be drastically reduced. There could be no social justification for a situation in which about 1 per cent of the population own about 40 per cent of all personal net capital and about 5 per cent of the population own between two-thirds and three-quarters of all personal property. The *Declaration of Dissent* said that the Government's incomes policy would help to peipetuate this inequality.

The *Declaration of Dissent* challenged the contention that British exports were held back because of the high wages of British workers or the rapid rate of improvement in British working conditions. Figures were quoted from a number of sources to show that wage rates were not high in Britain in comparison with most other industrial countries, and that wages and working conditions in Britain were improving more slowly than elsewhere.

The *Declaration of Dissent* pointed out that Britain's military burden was far too heavy and that at least half the deficit on the balance of payments was accounted for by overseas military expenditure. This, it said, was indefensible. Military expenditure should be drastically reduced.

The *Declaration of Dissent* emphasised that adequate rewards were needed for training, skill and experience in British industry. The British economy, it said, had suffered because of the poor rewards it had provided to many who have scientific and technical skill. This would not be solved by observing the kind of incomes policy put forward by the Government.

New Measures

In February and April of 1965 the Government issued two further white papers outlining the machinery which they proposed to establish to review particular movements in prices and incomes, and the general considerations that should apply, in conformity with the Government's incomes policy, to prices and incomes. The Government proposed to establish a Prices and Incomes Board to review particular cases affecting prices or incomes. These cases would be referred to the Prices and Incomes Board by the Government. In their April 1965 White Paper the Government said that it would be impracticable and undesirable to lay down detailed rules regarding wage and salary movements. Nevertheless, they said that a norm should be established to indicate the average rate of annual increases of money incomes per head consistent with stability in the general level of prices. This norm, appropriate for the then existing circumstances, was, they said, 3–3½ per cent. Exceptional pay increases should be confined to employees accepting more exacting work or a major change in working practices which resulted in a direct contribution towards increased productivity. Even in such cases some of the benefit would have to accrue to the community as a whole in the form of lower prices. Other exceptional cases were listed as: (a) where a pay increase was both necessary and effective for securing a change in the distribution of manpower or preventing a change which might otherwise take place; (b) where there was general recognition that existing wage and salary levels were too low to maintain a reasonable standard of living; (c) where there was widespread recognition that the pay of a certain group of workers had fallen seriously out of line with the level of remuneration for similar work.

These steps proved to be inadequate to fulfil the Government's purpose. In the beginning of September 1965 the Government announced their intention to seek statutory power to introduce a compulsory "early warning" system for prices and incomes. They said that they would take power to require advance notification of any intended increase in prices or charges or claims relating to pay, hours or other major improvements and any prospective terms of settlement in such cases. Since clearly it was not possible to introduce immediate legislation for such powers the Government sought the co-operation of the TUC and the Confederation of British Industry for a voluntary "early warning" system. This co-operation was subsequently given.

In July 1966 the Government announced more stringent measures to enforce their incomes policy. On 20 July, in the House of Commons, the Prime Minister said that money incomes had been increasing at a rate far faster than could be justified by increasing production. Britain was again faced with a very serious balance of payments problem and the country, he said, needed a breathing space of 12 months in which productivity could catch up with the excessive increases in incomes which had taken place. The Government proposed, therefore, to introduce a standstill on prices and incomes.

The standstill on incomes was more rigid than on prices. According to the Government's White Paper exemptions for price increases were given to the extent that "increases in prices or charges may be necessary because of marked increases which cannot be absorbed in costs of imported materials, or which arise from changes in supply for seasonal or other reasons, or which are due to action by the Government such as increased taxation". In relation to incomes the Government said that there should be a standstill on all increases up to the end of 1966 except normal arrangements for increasing pay either with age, as with apprentices or juveniles, or by means of regular increments of specified amounts within a predetermined range or scale. The period of standstill, which was to last until the end of 1966, was, according to the Government, to be followed by a 6-month period of "severe restraint". The standstill was not intended to apply to increases in pay resulting directly from increased output or increases in pay genuinely resulting from promotion to work at a higher level. It did, however, apply to commitments which had been entered into, on or before 20 July 1966, but which had not yet been implemented. These commitments included agreements to increase pay from an operative day before, on or after 20 July, pay increases due under cost-of-living sliding scale arrangements and commitments to review pay or hours from a date already agreed on or before 20 July 1966. The Government said that the incomes norm during the period of severe restraint, i.e. the first 6 months of 1967, must be regarded as zero.

The Prime Minister also indicated on 20 July that new legislation would be introduced to ensure that the Government had adequate powers to enforce its policy. The proposed legislation for the "early warning" system was to be widened to include a new section which would give the Government power to make Orders directing that specified prices or charges or specified rates of wages and salaries should not be increased without Ministerial consent. These provisions were to be for a limited period only.

Legislation

The amended version of the Prices and Incomes Bill was passed by Parliament in the late summer of 1966. In addition to providing a statutory basis for the Prices and Incomes Board and the examination of movements in prices and incomes referred to the Board by the Government, the Act also contained the special temporary provisions outlined by the Government in their emergency statement in July 1966. Under Part IV of the Prices and Incomes Act the Government were empowered not only to enforce a temporary standstill on prices and particular levels of remuneration but also they were given power to reverse price or pay increases implemented after 20 July 1966. The appropriate Minister was empowered to direct that any specified price or charge should be reduced to a level not lower than that prevailing on or before 20 July 1966. The persons affected by such a direction were to be given 14 days' notice of it and the Minister was required to consider any representations made to him within this time. The Act also gave legal immunity to employers who, in response to the Government's request for a standstill, voluntarily withheld pay increases to which an employee was entitled under his contract of employment. In other words the Prices and Incomes Act gave legal protection to employers to break contracts of employment in order to observe the requirements of the Government's policy (although, for various reasons, very few employers took the necessary legal steps to protect themselves). Part IV of the Act was not invoked until ASSET took legal action, through a representative member, against Thorn Electrical Industries to secure money due under a contract and withheld allegedly in deference to the Government's policy. ASSET eventually won the case. The Government had sought to exceed the powers given to them by law.

The Prices and Incomes Act, 1966, introduced a number of new features into industrial relations which are in every way objectionable from the standpoint of trade unionists. In the first place the Act can require the deferment of the implementation of settlements freely reached between employers and trade unions. This deferment can take place quite apart from the temporary provisions in the Act which empower the Government to interfere directly in wage settlements. Secondly, the Act introduces a new criminal liability

on workers who threaten to take any action with a view to
compelling, inducing, or influencing an employer to implement an
award or settlement in respect of employment at a time when the
implementation of that award or settlement has been forbidden by
the Government. A person convicted under this provision is liable
to be fined. A trade union can also be charged under this section
and it too can be fined. Presumably if a person found guilty under
this section failed to pay the fine imposed upon him he would be
liable to imprisonment for contempt of court. Thirdly, the temporary provisions of the Act enabled the Government not only to
defer wage or other settlements but also to prohibit them. This
was an extremely dangerous precedent. Fourthly, the temporary
provisions in the Act gave legal immunity to employers to break
contracts of employment in response to the requirements of the
Government's policy. This too was unprecedented in British
history.

Severe Restraint

In November 1966 the Government issued a further white paper
setting out the basic considerations to be observed during the
period of severe restraint during the first 6 months of 1967. It was
once again emphasised that the norm for the annual rate of increase in money incomes per head must be zero. Increases in
incomes could be justified, it said, only in exceptional cases and
even then only on a severely limited scale. The exceptions listed
concerned employees who make a direct contribution towards increasing productivity by accepting, for example, more exacting
work or a major change in working practices. Even then some of
the benefits should accrue to the community as a whole in the
form of lower prices or improvements in quality. The second
exception outlined in the white paper was for the "worst off"
members of the community. It would be necessary to ensure, however, said the white paper, that any pay increases justified on this
ground were genuinely confined to the lowest paid workers and
not passed on to other workers.

On 2 March 1967 the TUC convened a conference of trade union executive committees to consider the latest developments on incomes policy. The policy statement put forward by the General Council of the TUC was in many ways critical of the policy of the Government. The General Council said that an effective incomes policy was not possible except in the context of an effective economic and social plan. Such a plan should include as essential objectives the improvement of real wages and salaries and the redress of inequities in the distribution of income and wealth. The General Council stated, however, that whatever differences of view had emerged between the Government and the TUC the General Council still believed that the Government's long-term objectives were not in their essentials different from those of the TUC.

The General Council said that they were convinced that an incomes policy could not be enforced on reluctant trade unionists by legislation. They explained that in their view Part IV of the Prices and Incomes Act, which was due to lapse in August 1967, should not be renewed or replaced by any similar provisions, and that it was neither necessary nor desirable to implement the part of the Act which provided for the establishment of a statutory "early warning" system. The General Council urged that priority should continue to be given to encouraging settlements which promoted productivity and to improving the position of low paid workers (which, they explained, was significantly different from the concept of "lowest paid" outlined in the Government's white paper).

The statement of policy issued by the General Council of the TUC said that if trade unionists continued to accept and even assert the desirability of a planned and progressive incomes policy they must accept the consequent obligation to ensure that their own actions did not impede the achievement of full employment, economic expansion, rising living standards and the more equitable distribution of income and wealth to which they themselves accorded priority. An acceptable incomes policy must, therefore, be part of a plan for national economic expansion.

The General Council of the TUC said that no Government was competent to interfere in detail in collective bargaining without causing disruption. The TUC itself, therefore, would have to adopt a more positive approach to the development of an acceptable incomes policy if it were to be able to convince the Government that the collective action of unions would not prevent the achievement of national objectives.

The General Council said that they intended to issue towards the end of each year an annual report on the economic situation and prospects for the ensuing year. This report would incorporate the General Council's views on the general level of increases in wages and salaries that would be appropriate in the ensuing year, and on the kinds of circumstances which would justify deviations from the general level. This general report would be considered by a conference of the executives of affiliated unions to be held early in the following year. This step, it was explained, would in itself constitute a significant advance towards a co-ordinated trade union incomes policy. The unions would also be expected, as previously, to notify the TUC of all claims under consideration relating to improvements in wages and working conditions. The unions, it was said, would be expected to refrain from proceeding with claims until they had received the observations of the Incomes Policy Committee of the General Council of the TUC. Unions would be expected to take account of those observations in deciding whether to proceed with their claims. Unions would also be expected to notify the TUC of the terms of any settlements reached with employers.

Finally, the General Council stated that trade unionists were not interested in an incomes policy which was based on the assumption that the share of the national income going to working people would remain the same. Their interest, it was said, lay in a radical and progressive incomes policy which would increase their share of the nation's wealth.

The policy statement of the General Council of the TUC was put to the conference of trade union executive committees on 2 March. The two authors of this book were among the delegates who spoke in opposition to the General Council's statement. The main arguments they advanced were as follows:

(1) That the reality of the economic situation was very different from that which the General Council said was necessary for an acceptable incomes policy. There was not an effective social plan, there had been a growth of unemployment, production was stagnant, living standards had not improved and there had been no moves towards a more equitable distribution of wealth and income.

(2) That, though the General Council had said that a legally enforced incomes policy was not what was wanted, this, in fact, was what was promised by the Government. Restrictive legislation was to remain, and the Government had given no indication that they intended to restore the freedom of voluntary collective bargaining.

(3) That the trade union movement needed a much more radical approach to the inequalities of British society. Millions of people were living at a standard below that set by the National Assistance Board and there had been no significant change in recent years in the unequal distribution of income and wealth.

(4) That the Government were pursuing a foreign policy which required them to spend substantial sums on the maintenance of troops and bases abroad. This was a major cause of Britain's recurring balance of payments problem.

(5) That it was the Government's deflationary measures and not the freedom of unions to bargain collectively which had caused unemployment. Hence it was the Government's policy that needed to be changed and not trade union rights to be curtailed.

Despite these arguments the report of the General Council of the TUC was adopted by an overwhelming majority. The voting was 7,604,000 for the report and 963,000 against.

Permanent Legislation?

Any hope that the Government would abandon its restrictive legislation on incomes was dispelled by the publication in March 1967 of a new white paper entitled *Prices and Incomes Policy after 30th June, 1967*. This white paper explained that, though Part IV of the Prices and Incomes Act would lapse on 11 August 1967, the Government intended to bring Part II into operation. They announced that they would be consulting further with the CBI and the TUC about what they described as "a limited development of the reserve powers over prices and incomes under the Prices and Incomes Act 1966". This clearly foreshadowed not a weakening but a strengthening of the permanent provisions of the Prices and Incomes Act.

The white paper also made it very clear that there was no justification in the Government's view for returning to the norm of 3–3½ per cent per annum for increases in incomes which prevailed up to July 1966. The white paper said that over the 12-month period beginning 1 July 1967, no one could be entitled to a minimum increase. Any proposed increase or other significant improvement in conditions would need to be justified against criteria set out in the white paper. These criteria were those set out in the earlier white paper entitled *Prices and Incomes Policy* published in April 1965. Less regard, it was said, should be paid to such factors as general comparisons with incomes in other employments and changes in the cost of living. Moreover, in applying the criteria certain additional considerations should be taken into account. Twelve months should be regarded as the minimum period between the operative dates of successive improvements for any group of workers. In some cases substantial improvements in pay or conditions, which might be justified under the criteria, should be achieved not in one stage but by stages. Finally, the unions, it was said, should not seek to make good increases foregone as a result of the standstill and severe restraint.

In the White Paper *Prices and Incomes Policy after 30th June, 1967*, the Government argued that the emergency measures taken in July 1966 had had considerable success. The balance of payments had improved, sterling had been greatly strengthened, the excess pressure of demand at home had been eliminated, resources had been freed for export production and other essential purposes and the rise in prices and incomes had been slowed down.

All this, of course, is a familiar part of the stop–go cycle. It was, therefore, ironic that the Government should justify these deflationary measures on the grounds that they were hoping to create conditions favourable to sustained economic growth. The plain fact is that, though the Labour Party was elected on a programme of economic expansion, the industrial output figures have barely increased since 1964. The improvement in the balance of payments was secured as a result of stop–go policies similar to those pursued on previous occasions. The wheels of production were slowed down and the balance of payments gap narrowed. There is nothing unique about this experience. It has been tried all before by Conservative governments during their period of rule between 1951 and 1964.

The new legislation to strengthen the Government's incomes policy was introduced and passed by Parliament in the summer of 1967. It was the Prices and Incomes (No. 2) Act. It supplemented the power of the Government under Part II of the Prices and Incomes Act 1966 to impose standstills on increases in prices or pay. In cases where there is an adverse report by the National Board for Prices and Incomes the standstill may be extended for a period up to six months. The new Act also gave legal immunity to employers who withheld pay increases due before or during the period 20 July 1966 to 1 July 1967.

The Alternative

Part of the real alternative to the Government's policies was outlined in a resolution adopted by the 1966 Labour Party Conference despite the opposition of the platform. This resolution was moved by the TGWU. Its terms were as follows:

> This Conference recognises that unless there is a substantial reduction in military expenditure the Labour Government's ability to achieve the

national economic recovery, social progress and prosperity to which it is pledged, will be impeded by recurring balance of payments crises.

Conference calls upon the Government to contract its role in Western Germany, and make a decisive reduction in military commitments East of Suez, including the withdrawal from Malasia, Singapore and the Persian Gulf, by 1969–1970, thus ending excessive strain on the armed forces and over-dependence on American support and making possible a defence budget well below £1,750 million.

Recognition of the crippling effect of Government overseas spending on Britain's economic position has not been confined to the left wing of the Labour Movement. People of widely differing views, both in the Conservative Party and the Labour Party, have pointed to the fact that Britain does not suffer from a trade deficit but from a balance of payments deficit.* In an article, for example, in the *Sunday Times* of 2 October 1966, one of Britain's leading bankers, Sir Siegmund Warburg, pointed out that between 1952 and 1964 Government expenditure overseas increased nearly sevenfold to a peak of £549,000,000 per annum. This steady increase in Government spending, which had not been matched by a similar increase in private sector earnings, had resulted in the deterioration in Britain's position with which the public were now only too familiar. Table 3 was published as part of Sir Siegmund Warburg's article.

Unfortunately the Defence white paper published in July 1967 indicates clearly that the Government have no intention of fulfilling the terms of the 1966 Labour Party conference resolution. By the mid-1970's(!) it is hoped that the military budget may be reduced to £1800 million at 1964 prices. Even if this is achieved it is much too small a cut and much too late.

* Readers who are interested in more detailed discussion of the balance of payments problem should refer to the book *The Problem of Sterling* by A. R. Conan, published by MacMillan. The author concluded, after a most detailed examination of the position, that there was not a persistent or exceptional weakness in Britain's balance of payments except in relation to Government overseas expenditure. Only the large Government debit, said Mr. Conan, had proved intractable. He added: "on the whole the results for the purely economic categories may be regarded as good and weakness can be only insofar as they are offset by an ever rising total of Government expenditure."

The problem thus is one primarily for the Government. All the attention which has been focused on the question of incomes policy is to a considerable extent a diversion. The real need is not to restrain allegedly aggressive trade unions and to take away traditional rights of working people but to cut substantially Government overseas spending and to plan for expansion at

TABLE 3. HOW GOVERNMENT SPENDING HIT THE TRADE BALANCE

	Visible trade balance (£ million)	Invisible balance (private sector)			Net government overseas expenditure (current and cap.)	Trade balance + government expenditure
1956	+ 53	+ 330	=	+ 383	− 243	+ 140
1957	− 29	+ 396	=	+ 367	− 78	+ 289
1958	+ 29	+ 526	=	+ 555	− 269	+ 286
1959	− 118	+ 481	=	+ 363	− 351	+ 12
1960	− 408	+ 416	=	+ 8	− 386	− 378
1961	− 153	+ 481	=	+ 328	− 378	− 50
1962	− 104	+ 566	=	+ 462	− 465	− 3
1963	− 83	+ 573	=	+ 490	− 488	+ 2
1964	− 543	+ 583	=	+ 40	− 549	− 509
1965	− 280	+ 632	=	+ 352	− 540	− 188

United Kingdom Balance of Payments, 1966 (Central Statistical Office).

home. Within a planned economy, with industrial expansion, full employment, steadily advancing living standards and the re-distribution of income and wealth in favour of those who work and against those who live primarily by ownership, an incomes policy would make sense. It does not make sense when its purpose is to accommodate excessive Government overseas spending, primarily for military purposes, and when it forms part of a wider policy of economic stop–go and the maintenance of the gross inequality which at present disfigures British society.

In September 1967 the British trade union movement gave its answer to the Government's policies. By a majority of 1,381,000 the TUC adopted the following resolution:

> This Congress deplores the use by the Government of traditional deflationary measures to manage the economy which involve the creation of a pool of un-employed workers, and have the effect of weakening our economic base and worsening our world competitive position. Congress rejects the Government's intervention in collective bargaining as a solution to the country's economic problems. It is of the opinion that the role of Government should be one of creating the right economic conditions and therefore calls for adequate planning of national assets involving the full use of all indigenous resources.
>
> To this end the Government should seek to:
> (i) maintain full employment;
> (ii) effectively control both the import and export of capital;
> (iii) increase its efforts with regard to world trade and development;
> (iv) drastically reduce military expenditure;
> (v) limit and stabilise prices, rents, dividends and profits;
> (vi) increase efficiency and productivity and encourage recognition of trade unions by all sections of trade and industry.
>
> Congress believes that such actions are urgent and is convinced that any plan for economic progress resulting in a real growth of wages and salaries can only be achieved by an extension of public ownership which it considers vital to any national economic plan.

In Conclusion

Our view is a simple one. The unions are underprivileged and their members—who comprise the producers of wealth and the inspirers of progress in these islands—are divorced from the power and denied the gains they deserve.

We want to set in motion events which will change all this. We offer the suggestions for limited reform contained in these chapters as a primer to the powder.

Index